1095

THE PUBLICITY AND PROMOTION HANDBOOK

THE PUBLICITY AND PROMOTION HANDBOOK

A COMPLETE GUIDE FOR SMALL BUSINESS

Linda Carlson

CBI Publishing Company, Inc.
51 Sleeper Street   Boston, MA 02210

Production Editor: Kathy Savago
Interior Design: Lifland et al., Bookmakers
Cover Design: MaryEllen Podgorski
Compositor: A & B Typesetters

Library of Congress Cataloging in Publication Data

Carlson, Linda C.
  The publicity and promotion handbook.

  1. Small business. 2. Industrial publicity. 3. In-
dustrial promotion. I. Title.
HD2341.C35   659.2′81   81-10060
ISBN 0-8436-0865-X   AACR2

Printing (last digit): 9 8 7 6 5 4 3 2

Printed in the United States of America

For my grandparents

CONTENTS

ACKNOWLEDGMENTS

I don't trust people who claim that writing books is a pleasure, an effortless diversion. I am a writer—by training, by inclination, by sheer love of language—and I found this book a monumental challenge. Helping me through the months of research and the pressured weeks of writing were countless people: the men and women who answered my questions about the benefits of publicity, the instructors and fellow students at the Harvard Business School, old friends in Washington State University's journalism program, colleagues at the American Plywood Association and at Bendix (now American) Forest Products Corporation, magazine editors across the country, and the staff at CBI.

My special thanks to Frank Anton, Howard Backen and Jim Mitchell, Jack Bloodgood, William Bruder, Ruth Kirk, Al Lees, Julie Ockfen, Lois Rich and Barbara Egerman, Frowis Roewer, Cheryl Scott, Paula Simmons, Diane Solvang-Angell, Bob Strode, Harry Wicks, and Oliver Witte. I am also grateful for the help of Shirley Walker, who converted my scrawled paragraphs into a presentable manuscript; to my parents, in whose lakeside cabin most of the writing was done; and, of course, to Pam Allsebrook, with whom this project was started.

PREFACE

You'll find no rhetoric, no lengthy philosophical discussions in this book. This is a "how to" guide, a "cookbook" that will walk you through every step of several different marketing projects. Besides explaining how to complete a project—whether it be a press release or a picture, an advertisement or an awards program entry—I've tried to tell you where to go for help and how much you can expect to spend.

This book is intended as a reference, as the guide you can pull off the shelf whenever you're not sure where to start with a plant tour, a press conference, or a photo filing system. This book is to be used; fill its margins with notes about what is most effective—and most economical—for your business and your community.

L.C.

1

AN
INTRODUCTION

There is nothing very complicated about public relations; like every other good business practice, it is based on common sense, courtesy, and a sense of what is special about your business's products and services.

Because people—employees and associates, distributors, bankers, competitors, editors, and, of course, customers—are an important part of every business, they are also an important part of every public relations activity. Whether you are writing a press release or returning a telephone call, designing a brochure or decorating your office, you are telling people something about you and the way you run your business, your products and services, and your industry.

Because public relations allows you to communicate so much information, it is a valuable marketing tool. Before people ever see your product catalog, hear your presentation, or meet your sales representative, you can use public relations to tell potential customers who you are, what you do, how well you do it, how much you charge, and why they need you. Public relations does not replace advertising or personal selling; it makes them more effective. Through public relations you can introduce a new product to the public before the first advertisement appears; you can prepare a potential customer for the sales representative's first call. You can show current customers new products and services as well as new applications of existing products and services; you can reassure new customers and encourage them to buy again.

WHAT IS PUBLIC RELATIONS?

Public relations is a press release, a speech, a slide presentation, a factory tour. It is the brochure on your work, the displays in your office, the note you write to an editor, the well-cropped photographs of your projects, and the holiday open house in your office. Public relations can be as complex as a year-long publicity campaign complete with press conferences and talk show appearances; it can be as simple as hiring a cheerful receptionist to answer your telephone and greet your visitors.

WHAT DOES PUBLIC RELATIONS DO?

Although the results of public relations activities are, like those of advertisements, often difficult to measure, many firms have discovered that carefully planned public relations programs can yield extraordinary results. Some public relations efforts are ego boosters; they have no immediate effect on your business, but they send you home proud of your first speech or your first appearance on a radio talk show. Other activities start your telephone ringing and bring you inquiries and clients within days. For example, when Richard Sygar's design work was featured in a two-page *New York Times* story about young designers, he received more than a dozen calls from prospective clients within ten days. Charles Hughes, another designer, cited in the same story, was offered (and accepted) a job with a large architectural firm as a result of the publicity. When pictures of a house built from a Backen Arrigoni & Ross design were published in *Hudson Home Magazine*, the San Francisco architects received several orders for the house plans. When a vacation house he had designed was featured in *Sunset*, Arizona architect William Bruder received 100 calls and letters.

Design firms are not the only businesses to benefit from public relations. When Lois Rich and Barbara Egerman's "supersisters" baseball-style cards about prominent women were mentioned in a lengthy *Ms.* article about toys, 500 *Ms.* readers immediately placed orders. The *Ms.* comment about the Bear Essentials Toy Co. brought Marilyn Wenker many compliments and requests for catalogs. Although Wenker received no immediate orders as a result of the publicity, her sales representatives were delighted with the national coverage.

Mimi Gormezano's conversations with publicists and editors at an Association of Cooking Schools convention led to an assignment for a condiment manufacturer and a feature in *Cuisine* on Gormezano's cooking school. Because weaver Paula Simmons knew the editor of *Handweaver*, the magazine asked her for a series of articles on raising black sheep and using their wool. First published in 1962, these articles led to other writing assignments, to television appearances, to a series of books—and to a business that has grown steadily through the years without one line of paid advertising.

WHAT DOES PUBLIC RELATIONS REQUIRE?

As these examples show, a public relations program does not have to be time-consuming or expensive. You can handle many of the activities described in this book with only a few hours of time each week. How much you spend will depend on what you do. Printing a product catalog may cost several thousand dollars; writing press releases and organizing a slide program of existing photography can cost almost nothing. You do not need a full-time publicist or the help of an advertising or public relations agency. As your public relations activities increase and your firm grows, you may want staff help or consultants, but you do not need them for most of the activities you will read about here.

You need to know which people you want to reach and what you want to tell them. Start a list of all the possible means of bringing your message to these people; for example, you can write a press release or give a speech, print a brochure or run an ad. Jot down what information, equipment, and help each of these activities requires. To issue press releases you need an idea of what topics are appropriate and a review of basic journalistic style. You also need to know which publications might print a press release about your firm and where you can have the press releases duplicated. To give a speech, you need an audience, a topic, and some suggestions on public speaking. For a brochure or advertisement, you need a design, copy, and artwork.

How will you find all of these? That's what this book is for. In the pages that follow you will find examples of what other business people have tried, suggestions for your own public relations program, and lists of books, classes, products, and services you'll find helpful.

2

WHAT'S NEWS?
NEARLY EVERYTHING

What's news? Nearly everything that affects you and the people you know. When your sixth grader wins the election for class president, it's news to you and to her classmates. When you change jobs, it's news to the people with whom you work. When you open a business, it's news to the other merchants in town, to your potential customers, to suppliers, to tax officials, to labor leaders, and to people looking for jobs. When you introduce a product, it's news to your customers and your competitors, your dealers and your suppliers.

This chapter will help you determine what's newsworthy about you and your business and which publications will be interested in stories about you. You'll also find suggestions on when to submit your news stories and some hints on working with editors.

NEWS IS NEW INFORMATION

News is new information, the facts and figures and photographs that people haven't seen before. And it's important information; it's the facts and figures and photographs that people want to see. The newer the information and the more important it is to people, the more newsworthy the story. The more newsworthy the story, the more press and broadcast coverage it will receive. For example, the fact that you hired a different general manager a year ago is no longer news; he has been on the job so long that everyone who works with your firm has met him. The fact that he's speaking at the Chamber of Commerce next week is news; the information is new and it is important to Chamber members and other business people in your community. If he announces that you're automating your factory and laying off half your workers, his speech is very newsworthy; he's providing new information that directly affects your employees, your customers, your suppliers, and your community's tax and welfare agencies.

Look for news in everything you do, in everyone you see. As you read newspaper and magazine stories about businesses, as you listen to the radio and watch television, think about what makes every story newsworthy. In some stories, the people are newsworthy; in other stories, it's the products and services, the company's facilities, or its financial performance. What makes the people in your business newsworthy? Let's start with you. Are you a hometown kid coming back to take over or start a business? Is your work experience or your education unusual? Are you changing careers? Have you

been appointed or elected to an office in your trade or professional association? Think about the people who work with
you. Do you have a new partner? Or is one of your partners
leaving to start his or her own firm? Have you recently hired
or fired people? Who has been promoted? Who's retiring? Do
you have students who are receiving academic credit for
working with you? Maybe your work force isn't typical;
maybe you employ more young people, more older people, or
more part-timers than anyone else in town. Will you be hiring
people soon? Or is a lay-off coming?

Think about achievement, too. What have your firm and
your people accomplished recently? Have you received
awards from magazines, trade associations, or manufacturers? Have you presented awards to your employees, your
distributors, or your sales representatives?

Have you presented scholarships to your employees or to
their children? Have your employees recently completed
training programs or college classes? Has the firm been
recognized by the media—by a trade journal or a consumer
magazine, by a radio talk show or a television commentary?

What is newsworthy about your products and services?
Are they interesting because they're new? Because you use
uncommon materials and methods? Because they're much
less (or much more) expensive than anything comparable?
You are newsworthy if you meet very special needs—if you
cater meals to diabetics or run gubernatorial campaigns, if
you design special tools for the blind or prefabricate
buildings that can be erected atop rugged mountains.

How do you sell your products and services? Do you test
market? Do you advertise? Are you changing advertising
campaigns and slogans? Are you switching from television to
print? Or from billboards to direct mail? Have you withdrawn
a product from the market? Do you face a product recall?

Are you moving your office? That's newsworthy, too.
What's your new address? Have you purchased a building or
are you constructing one? Is the building a historical land-
mark? How many other tenants will there be? Is the building
all leased or is there space available?

What are you doing to decrease energy consumption? Are you renovating the building or adding on to improve working conditions and capacity? Have you installed a new assembly line? Do you have new environmental protection equipment? Is your production being affected by a shortage of raw materials and skilled labor or the increasing cost of water and energy?

If your firm is publicly owned, your financial performance is newsworthy. Have your sales and earnings increased or declined in the last year? In the last quarter? Are you selling more stock or have you just had a stock split? Have you increased or cut dividends? Have you sold bonds?

What your company does in the community is newsworthy, too. Have you or your employees donated time, money, or materials to charities, civic projects, or schools? Do you offer factory or office tours to schoolchildren, civic groups, your employees' families, elected officials, and important visitors to your community? Do you sponsor company picnics and banquets? Do you and the people who work for you give speeches at meetings of community and professional groups?

WHO IS INTERESTED IN YOUR NEWS?

Now you know what is newsworthy about you and your business. The next question: who's interested in a story about you? Start with the people who know you and the people who work for you. What happens to your business is also important to the people who buy your products, the people who supply your raw materials, the people who finance you, and the people who compete with you. Don't forget the unions and guilds whose members work for you and the local officials who depend on your tax payments.

How do you get news about yourself to these people? To reach the people in your community, use the publications they read, the radio programs they hear, and the television news programs they watch. For example, in Seattle people

read the daily *Post-Intelligencer* and the *Seattle Times;*
business people read the *Journal of Commerce,* the *Seattle
Business Journal,* and the western edition of the *Wall Street
Journal.* People who live in well-defined neighborhoods read
weekly community papers like the *Queen Anne News* and the
Capitol Hill Times. To see what's on sale at the True Value or
Rexall, they glance through the "shoppers" that are dis-
tributed free to nearly every home. For in-depth stories on
the arts and local events, they read the *Argus* and the
Weekly. For features on entertaining, gardening, and vaca-
tioning in their area, they read the northwest edition of
Sunset.

People in your community aren't the only ones who will
be interested in you and your business. To reach people
across the country or around the world, look into regional,
national, and international newspapers and magazines; companies' own publications; and the newsletters sent by subscription only to people in special professions and industries.
The magazines that feature small and large businesses include news magazines like *Time* and *Newsweek*; shelter
magazines like *Better Homes and Gardens* and *House &
Garden;* regional magazines like *Boston, Houston,* and *San
Diego;* and business publications like *Fortune, Forbes,
Business Week,* and the *Wall Street Journal.* Many publications serve only small groups of business people: *Inc.* is written for small business owners and *Savvy* for women in
business. *Professional Builder* is written for developers,
Stores for retailers, *Restaurant Hospitality* for restaurateurs,
the *Nevada Rancher* for cattle ranchers, *Savings and Loan
News* for bankers, and *Playthings* for people who sell toys
and crafts.

Some editors are interested in you because they write
about people like yourself. The editors of *Progressive Architecture* and *Architectural Record* want stories about architects; the editors of *Housing, Builder,* and *Professional
Builder* want stories about developers; the editors of *Savings
Bank Journal* and *Credit Union Magazine* want stories about
thrift institutions.

Other editors are interested in you because they write for the people who use your products and services. If you sell school furniture or advise school boards on federal aid, the editors of *American School and University* are interested in you. If you sell forklift trucks or pallets, the editors of *Modern Materials Handling* find you newsworthy. If you sell greenhouse plans or portable power tools, the editors of *Popular Mechanics* and *Popular Science* are interested in you.

To determine which publications might be interested in you, make two lists. On the first, write the name of every magazine that is written for people like you. On the second, list the magazines written for your potential customers. As you make the lists, think of yourself in the broadest possible sense. If you're a woman running a small accounting firm, put *Savvy, Working Woman,* and *Ms.* on your first list. Add *Cosmopolitan, Glamour,* and *Redbook.* You operate a small business, so include *Inc.* You're an accountant, so remember *Practical Accountant, Woman CPA* and your state accounting magazine. Now add your college alumni publication, your church newsletter, and the newspapers and magazines that circulate in the city where you live.

For your second list, think about the people you would like to have as customers. Every business needs income tax returns, balance sheets, and profit and loss statements, so every business is a potential customer. So are the individuals with complicated tax returns, stock and bond portfolios, weekend farms, or other personal business matters. When you have decided which of these businesses and individuals you want to reach, list the business publications and trade journals that are written for them. Now add the names of those general interest magazines and newspapers with special columns and sections on business. To find which magazines serve which special interest groups, use the directories on file at your library's reserve desk. For the names of directories you'll want to consult, see Appendix A.

Take your list to the local library and study the magazines in which you're interested. How do they differ in the topics they cover? In the length of the stories? In the amount of background information? In objectivity? In the number and quality of pictures? Because each editor is striving to reach a slightly different group of readers, you will see that the same news stories are treated in many different ways and that each publication uses a different combination of stories and pictures.

WHEN TO SUBMIT NEWS

Knowing when to send information on your business to an editor is as important as knowing where to send it. Most metropolitan newspapers are published daily, but editors often save stories for the special sections that are published once a week, once a month, or once a year. For example, the *New York Times* publishes its "Home" section on Thursdays and "Weekend" on Fridays. The *Los Angeles Times* publishes a business section on Tuesdays, a food section on Thursdays, and fashion features on Fridays. The Flint, Michigan, *Journal* runs home improvement stories every Friday, and the Columbus, Ohio, *Dispatch* features travel on Sundays. These sections, especially if they are part of Sunday editions, are edited and sometimes printed days before the rest of the issue. An editor may want the stories for the Sunday women's page submitted by Wednesday; a weekly that lists Thursday as its day of publication may actually be printed Tuesday night or Wednesday morning, so the editor will need your story by Monday afternoon. To obtain newspaper deadlines and the names of special sections and editions, call the business, city, or managing editors of your local publications. Add the deadlines to your list of newspapers and magazines; call the editors every year or so to update the information.

Magazines also have special issues. *Professional Builder* features California developments every June; *Architectural Records* presents award-winning houses and apartments in a special mid-May issue. *Builder* features the National Association of Home Builders show in January, new products in

February, and Gold Nugget award winners every June. Most consumer magazines run Christmas stories in December and vacation suggestions in May or June.

To find out what editors plan to feature in each issue, ask them if they prepare editorial calendars. Sometimes called publishing plans, these schedules allow both the editorial and advertising staffs to work as much as eighteen months in advance. At some magazines, especially trade journals, editorial calendars are published and distributed to sales representatives, scouts, publicists, and advertisers; you can obtain copies of the plans by simply writing or calling editors. At magazines where detailed publishing plans are not prepared, editors will often tell you what they plan to feature in the next five or six issues. At other magazines, editorial calendars are prepared in detail, department by department, but they are not printed or even discussed with people other than the staff members. However, if you describe a specific project or product to an editor at one of these magazines, he or she will tell you if your material is appropriate for a future issue.

Use the printed editorial calendars, the notes you make during telephone conversations with editors, and an idea of each magazine's deadlines to put together a schedule for submitting information and developing or finding projects that meet editors' needs. For example, if you know that the staff at *Better Homes and Gardens* selects its Christmas stories a year in advance and starts to photograph the projects in May, you can submit your plans for toys, wreaths, or tree ornaments fourteen or eighteen months in advance of the issue. If you know that *Ms.* writers start research in February for their pre-Christmas feature on toys, you can make January your deadline for producing prototypes of your educational dolls. If you know that the editors at *Inc.* magazine will be starting work in the fall on a January issue on business management, you can spend the last week in August outlining the case history that you want to submit.

Remember that editors are serious about deadlines. The complexities of printing, binding, and mailing thousands— and often millions—of copies of a magazine require days and

FIGURE 2-1　EDITORIAL CALENDAR

even weeks. At Meredith Publishing in Des Moines, for example, three high-speed presses run around the clock for thirty days to produce the eight million copies of each issue of *Better Homes and Gardens*. Even before a magazine issue goes to the printer, there are weeks of work. Story topics are suggested and evaluated, often by the magazine or department's entire editorial staff. Charts and plans are drawn and photographs taken; color separations are made and headlines are written and typeset. Then the entire issue is carefully written and designed to make one story lead into another. Thus editors prefer to have most of their material in hand at the first planning meetings. Of course, when a late story is obviously more important than anything already planned for a issue, editors will make eleventh hour changes in copy and photographs. With most trade journals and consumer magazines, however, the last-minute story is left over—maybe to be used in the next issue. Because most publications are printed in busy plants where production deadlines are scheduled months in advance, printing deadlines are seldom changed to accommodate a late story or picture.

Careful attention to deadlines is one way to maintain a good relationship with editors. Make sure they can reach you when they need additional information, too; if you operate a one-person office, have a telephone answering service or machine to take calls when you're away. For suggestions on meeting editors and sending them material, see the next chapter.

3

THE
FEATURE
ARTICLE

Open up your favorite newspaper or magazine and you'll find articles on everything from antique clothes dealers and orchid nurseries to new housing developments and self-service automotive garages. How did these stories come about? How do the editors and reporters learn about new and existing products, projects, services, and firms? How can you make the right editor aware of you?

You'll find the answers in this chapter. You will learn how to meet editors and how to submit material to them; you will find an outline of what makes projects newsworthy; and you will see how other business people obtain the client permission that is necessary before a project is published. The chapter also shows how to handle simultaneous submittals and how to use publicity in your marketing program. Although it is written for every business person who would like publicity in newspapers and magazines, this chapter focuses specifically on the needs of designers.

MEET THE PRESS

Reporters and editors may find you. They may literally stumble over the new building you've designed or the new restaurant you're opening. More likely, they'll see your application for a building permit or liquor license. When they're preparing articles on antiques or orchids or self-service garages, they'll check the Yellow Pages or a city directory or call people who collect antiques or raise orchids.

Reporters and editors may also hear about you from the publicists who work for trade associations, manufacturers, and retailers. A trade association of building products manufacturers will send information on new projects using its materials to the editors of architectural, construction, and engineering journals. A manufacturer of sewing notions will send photographs of the place mats and pot holders you can make with its products to the editors of women's magazines and the columnists who write articles on sewing and crafts for newspaper syndicates. A chain of home improvement centers will send designs for bird feeders and barbecue pits to the editors of how-to and shelter magazines. The publicists will hear about you from their distributors or their sales representatives, or they'll find you when they are "scouting."

Besides relaying information about your product or services to editors, publicists may feature you in their own publications, advertisements, and sales literature. If you're working with a trade association, you may find information on you going to its members or to sister associations. To learn more about working with trade associations and manufacturers' publicity staffs, see Chapter 4.

There is one more way an editor may see your work. When you work on a construction, renovation, or decorating project that is being shot by a professional photographer, the photographer will probably send pictures and details of the project to editors of national trade and consumer magazines. For more information on working with photographers, see Chapter 7.

Take the Initiative

Of course, you don't have to wait for an editor or a publicist to find you. Getting your work into a magazine's pages is easiest when you've become acquainted with its editors, when you've learned what they need, and when they've learned that you are a dependable source of good stories. The first step is meeting the press.

Introduce yourself to reporters and editors at national conventions and trade shows. Even if you're not registered for the convention, you can often attend awards programs and cocktail parties. Because editors and public relations people will be registered, you will be able to identify them by the names on their badges. When you see someone who writes for a publication in which you would like publicity, don't hesitate to stop the editor by calling his or her name. If the editor is obviously hurrying to a meeting or is involved in an interview, make your introduction very short. "I'm Stephen Smith from Iowa City; I just wanted to say hello." Or, "I've been impressed by your recent columns on marketing." If the editor has time to talk, offer more information about your business and your work. Relate it to the magazine's recent articles. For example: "Mr. Murphy, I'm Beth Willis. I've been waiting for an opportunity to tell you how much I've enjoyed your recent features on interiors. We've been using many of the same nontraditional materials in our work in Berkeley. . . ."

You can also meet reporters and editors at local and regional conventions and trade shows and at receptions hosted by you or other business people to celebrate exhibitions, holidays, new offices, or new partners. You can call editors, too. If you are uncomfortable about a "cold" call, start the conversation with a compliment on a recent story or a question on an issue that is current in your industry. Quickly move the conversation to your work and your purpose in calling. "I'll be issuing a press release on our new partner next week and I want to know what your deadline is." Or, "We here at CSA Associates are organizing a public relations department, and I'm trying to find out how editors want project information submitted."

Get to know the consulting editors, the free-lance writers, the scouts, and the photographers who work closely with editors, too. Some publications have "stringers" in every major city; like scouts, these people send information to headquarters and select the projects that senior editors will visit when they make their annual visit to a region. Some magazines list these part-time employees on the masthead; others will give you their names and telephone numbers when you call the magazine office.

Follow-up Meetings and Calls

Follow up meetings and calls with notes describing your current projects. If you only had time to introduce yourself to an editor at a convention, you could follow the brief meeting with a note like this:

> How nice to meet you in Dallas! I'm sorry we didn't have more time to talk; I wanted to tell you about the shopping center I've been working on here in Spokane. The remodeling is only in its second phase, but the owners already have been able to double rents. And the merchants aren't complaining; their sales have increased at least twenty-five percent since. . . .

To write magazine editors, use the editorial office addresses listed near the front of each issue; to write trade associations and manufacturers, use the addresses in advertisements or on sales literature. Make your letters casual and friendly, but avoid colloquial expressions. Unless you know editors and publicists well enough to call them by their first names in conversation, don't do so in writing.

BEFORE YOU SUBMIT MATERIAL TO THE PRESS

If you have a project that you would like to have publicized, obtain your client's approval before submitting any information to the media or to publicists. Your clients may be concerned about privacy and security, and may have questions about endorsing your work and the materials that were used.

What can you do if your client is reluctant to have his or her project publicized? First, explain where you would like to send information on the project. Clients more often approve a submission when they understand who might be reading about them. To them, a particular publication's audience may seem so small or so specialized that they don't consider a story in that magazine enough exposure to threaten their security. If clients think that a publication's readership is too general to help their business, point out the special interest columns and the high circulation. For example, if you have refurbished the interiors of an old lodge, remind the innkeeper that such magazines as *Better Homes and Gardens, House Beautiful,* and *Cosmopolitan* publish travel columns. Each magazine is read by millions of people. Other clients may be delighted that you think their project is worthy of mention in magazines they respect. Some publicity-loving homeowners want pictures of their houses submitted to regional magazines like *Houston* and to glossy national publications like *Architectural Digest.*

To encourage a client to permit publicity, point out how other firms have benefited from coverage. Clients can use reprints of magazine and newspaper articles in their own promotional and recruiting campaigns. They can use favorable publicity, especially when the stories emphasize the challenges of the project, to explain high costs, lengthy construction periods, or extensive research and development programs to directors and shareholders. Corporate clients can mention award-winning buildings and publicly acclaimed programs in annual reports. Government officials can use media recognition of a new project or new services to obtain legislator and voter approval. Nonprofit groups can use media attention to dramatize their needs and develop a strong base of financial and political support.

You also can offer to submit the project to editors without the client's name, the project's address, or the construction cost. This is feasible for private homes and vacation houses. Several stories were published on a weekend retreat designed by Kirby Ward Fitzpatrick for a security-conscious couple; its location was never more specific than "northern California." In some magazines, owners' names and project locations are seldom mentioned.

If you promise your client anonymity, provide it. Do not include the client's name on any material sent to an editor or publicist; conceal any project identification like "Taylor house" if you send copies of the renderings or working drawings to the press.

A final argument: remind clients the publicity will help your business. If your clients are satisfied with your work, this alone may convince them to approve publicity.

When your clients do approve publicity, try to confirm this approval in writing. You can use a release form like Figure 3-1 or a letter like Figure 3-2. If you receive oral permission, write down the date and time of the conversation and the names of the participants. File this note with your project information.

I authorize John Jones to release pictures, plans, and information on Pine Meadows for use in awards program entries, news stories, and advertising material.

Name _____

Date _____

FIGURE 3-1   CLIENT RELEASE

Dear Mr. Brown:

I'm glad to hear you're willing to have Pine Meadows publicized.
I plan to submit information on the project to awards programs,
editors, manufacturers, and trade associations for possible
use in news stories and advertising material. I'll keep you
informed about the editors and publicists who express interest
in the project.

Sincerely,

John Jones

FIGURE **3-2** CLIENT RELEASE, SAMPLE LETTER

FINDING THE BEST AUDIENCE

Before you submit any material to an editor, think about the
people you want to reach. Now think about the magazines
these people read. If you don't know the names of every
magazine published for people in a particular industry or profession, use a directory like *Bacon's Publicity Checker.*
Bacon's and the similar directories listed in Appendix A are
available at the reserve desks of many public libraries.

Use a public or university library's collection of periodicals to skim the most recent copies of each magazine in
which you would like publicity. By studying the kind of articles each magazine publishes, you will learn whether the
editor wants stories on techniques or finished projects;
whether the magazine uses black-and-white pictures, color
photography, or drawings; and whether most articles are
written by the staff or by people like yourself. You'll also
learn which magazines share the same readers. For example,
the people who read the home improvement stories in *Sunset*
probably read *Popular Science* too. The people who read *Better Homes and Gardens'* car care columns probably read
Popular Mechanics's reviews of new cars. The people who
read features on interiors in *Progressive Architecture* and *Ar-*

chitectural Record probably read *Interiors* and *Interior Design.* Make a mental note of those magazines that appear to share the same readers for the same topics; these publications consider themselves competitors and you cannot submit material for the same feature story to them at the same time. As you study the magazines, think about your project and how it would fit into each of these publications. Don't send the editor of a how-to magazine a portfolio of beautiful 4 × 5-inch transparencies that show only the finished project. Don't send the editor of a picture book a nuts-and-bolts story on technique. Think about what makes your project newsworthy to different editors; if your project is a hotel, the editor of an architectural magazine may be interested in the design and the editor of an engineering magazine in the unusual construction techniques. An advertising magazine may want a story on the promotional campaign and a hospitality industry magazine a story on the facilities and services for conventions and meetings. As you gather the material you will submit to an editor, think about what is new or unusual about your project.

The high sales rate of a condominium project designed by Pomeroy Lebduska Associates and the problems presented by the site, a former junkyard bordered by a quarry and two prisons, attracted the attention of *Professional Builder* editors and resulted in a two-page feature in the magazine. Cabins designed to be constructed by their owners, all inexperienced carpenters, brought architect William Bruder publicity in magazine after magazine. Baseball cards have been traded for years, but cards with pictures and biographies of women achievers brought Lois Rich and Barbara Egerman's "supersisters" national media coverage. Paper dolls are another old idea, but Rinna Wolfe's dolls representing Jewish and black children were an unusual adaption that resulted in stories in local and national publications.

If you can identify a problem and describe how your product solves it, you probably have a story that will attract editors' attention. Because repair service is hard to find, for example, editors are interested in a woman who has taught

herself to restore cane furniture; because mortgage money is
often limited, editors look for examples of unusual financing
methods. Because more handicapped people are living and
working outside institutions, editors are interested in a
woman who designs clothes for people confined to wheelchairs. Because of the energy problem, editors want to know
more about a man who builds electric cars.

WHEN TO SUBMIT INFORMATION TO EDITORS

As you know from Chapter 2, some magazine editors start
planning an issue more than a year before it reaches the
newsstand. Other editors are still slipping in news notes and
black-and-white pictures a few weeks before the press date.
Whatever the policy, you will have the best opportunity for
publicity if you call or write an editor early, when he or she is
starting work on an issue.

Because each editor has a different work style and each
magazine has a different printing schedule, the length of the
planning cycle varies from one magazine to another. To determine when you should submit information to a particular
magazine, study its editorial calendar. It will list closing
dates for advertising, which is usually accepted for at least a
month longer than editorial material. Ask each editor how the
advertising and editorial closing dates differ for his or her
magazine. An editor at *Professional Builder* will probably tell
you that he or she wants to see your snapshots and a fact
sheet at least three months in advance of publication. If a
story on your project is accepted for publication, the photographer has a month to take the pictures; for the September
issue, the transparencies must be in the mail by the last week
of June. Black-and-white prints, which are easier to process
for reproduction, must be in the *Professional Builder* offices
by mid-July. At *Builder*, call or write the editor with your
story idea three or four months in advance. He or she will
want the professional color photography and art ten weeks
before publication and black-and-white pictures eight weeks
before the magazine comes out.

To submit a story to *Building Design & Construction*, another trade journal, you will have to start work a little earlier. Because all color photography must be in the editor's hands nearly three months in advance of publication, you should write your first letter at least four months in advance. *Better Homes and Gardens*, like most other consumer magazines, has a longer lead time; editors start planning a year or two in advance and send their material to the printer six months before the publication date. Quarterly special interest publications like *Better Homes and Gardens Remodeling Ideas* take nine months to write and print; the winter issue that goes on sale in late October is all written, photographed, and designed by early August, when production starts.

WHEN YOU CALL AN EDITOR

Should you call or write an editor? That all depends on the individual editor and the magazine. Some editors welcome a quick call followed by a package of information; others want pictures, plans, and a letter first.

If you've decided to call, try to do so when you can catch the editor in his or her office. Some New York editors don't get into their offices until 9:30 or 10 A.M. Others leave at 4 or 4:30 P.M. Some take two-hour or three-hour lunches. Still other editors spend very little time in their offices; one women's wear designer has said that she never tries to call a fashion editor after 9 A.M. or before 4 P.M. Outside New York, most editors have more conventional schedules. They may, however, have early morning staff meetings or interviews outside the office. Until you have an opportunity to ask editors when they prefer that you call, try between 9:30 and 11:30 A.M. and 2 and 4 P.M.

If you are calling across time zones, take advantage of off-peak long-distance rates. For example, if you call *Family Circle* in New York from San Francisco at 7:30 A.M., you reach the editor at 10:30 A.M. Eastern time and your call costs sixty percent less than if you had waited until 8 A.M. to call. If you

call *Architectural Digest* in Los Angeles from New York at
5:30 P.M., you reach the editor at 2:30 P.M.; your toll charge is
thirty-five percent less than it would have been before 5 P.M.

When you reach an editor, introduce yourself, explain
why you are calling, and always ask if he or she has a few
moments to talk. (You may be interrupting an interview,
another telephone conversation, a meeting with the art director, or a rush project.) For example, let's suppose you are a
builder who is finishing work on three custom houses that
might be appropriate for *Professional Builder*'s annual
custom housing issue. Six months in advance of the special
issue you call the editor and introduce yourself:

> Mr. Diaz, this is John Jones. I'm finishing construction of
> three homes I'd like you to consider for your custom housing
> issue. If you're free now I can tell you more about them. . . .

The editor asks for more information and you reply:

> They're all here in the Phoenix area, and they'll be completed
> within the next month or so. They range in size from a 1,500-
> square-foot retirement home for a widow to a 3,500-square-foot
> house for two attorneys and their four children. All the houses
> are contemporary, with wood siding, skylights, and solar
> heating units. Now the first one is particularly interesting
> because it was built around an elaborate fireplace that was
> saved when an old summer cabin was destroyed. . . .

In this conversation you've introduced yourself and
stated your purpose in calling. You've provided general information about the projects (their location, size, style, completion dates, materials, and examples of the clients) and started
to describe the special features of each house. To accomplish
this in writing, use a letter like Figure 3-3.

When you call an editor, have a mental list of the other
projects that you have been working on. Then you will be
prepared when an editor says, "Well, that isn't exactly what I
need now, but tell me what you're doing with small commercial buildings." Or with recycling. Or with marketing. When

Dear Mr. Diaz:

I've designed three custom houses that I want you to consider for your annual custom housing issue.

The houses all are contemporary; each has wood siding, skylights, and a solar heating system. All are being constructed in the Phoenix area and should be completed within six weeks. The enclosed fact sheet includes details on each project. I am also sending a slide of each house. If you would like additional information, I can be reached at (602) 987-6543.

When you no longer need the photographs, I would appreciate your returning them in the preaddressed envelope.

Sincerely,

John Jones

FIGURE 3-3 QUERY LETTER

an editor expresses interest in your project and asks for more information, send the additional details immediately. Tell the editor when you expect the project to be ready for professional (sometimes called "finish") photography.

TO SUBMIT INFORMATION

To submit information on a project, send the editor a one-page letter describing the project and your work. Indicate when and how you can be reached for more information. List or photocopy all enclosures; then, when you discuss the project with the editor, you will know exactly what material was sent. You will also have a record of where your pictures have been submitted. When the editor returns the photographs, you can check what has been returned against the photocopies or the enclosures listed on your copy of the letter. With the letter, send the following: color slides that you have taken yourself or duplicates of slides taken by a professional, or black-and-white or color prints; site and floor plans; drawings of any unusual details (for example, a section of an unusual wall system); and a fact sheet noting special problems, building and site size, construction materials, and construction

CONTACT:
Pamela Allsebrook
22 Napier Lane
San Francisco, California 94133
(415) 392-7880 (Office Phone)

SUBJECT: Sacramento, California
Suburban House Landscaping

PHOTOGRAPHER: Karl Riek
48 Second Street
San Francisco, California 94105
(415) 982-3419

LANDSCAPE   Robert M. Acrea
ARCHITECT: 6903 Tolura Lane
Citrus Heights, California 94105
(916) 445-3133 (Office Phone)

(Prefabricated greenhouse was installed by owner
after major landscaping was done. Owner does not
wish his name used.)

MATERIALS: Circular headers -- Redwood Clear All Heart
¼-inch benderboard, three pieces laminated.

Paving -- Pool and circular walkway accent
pieces are concrete aggregate. Pool paving
overhangs pool slightly. Driveway is brushed
concrete.

Trellising and decking -- Three basic trellised
areas, two off the wings of the house and one
separate unit by the pool. All are of redwood
Select Heart, 4 x 4-inch posts with 1 x 2s nailed
on each side. Decking is 2 x 6-inch redwood.
The trellising is stained charcoal gray to match
the house trim, and the decking is stained
medium brown to blend with the house siding.

Round deck -- Redwood Select Heart 2 x 6s stained
medium brown.

Greenhouse -- Prefabricated by
            Pacific Coast Greenhouse
             Manufacturing Company
            430 Hurlingame Avenue
            Redwood City, California 94063
            (415) 366-7672

Redwood with both plastic and glass panes -- redwood walkway and potting/shelf area in interior.
Approximately 10 x 20-foot dimension.

Fence surrounding backyard -- Rough-sawn garden
grade redwood 2 x 2s split into tri-stake
sections; 4 x 4-inch posts, approximately six
feet on center; and 2 x 4-inch crosspieces. Not
stained and will eventually weather to a driftwood
gray color.

FIGURE 3-4   FACT SHEET, SAMPLE 1

32

FIGURE **3-4** CONT.

DESIGN
CRITERIA:

The house is located at the end of a cul de sac.
It consists of a round living room/gallery with
two wings extending from the central section.
The bedroom area is on the right and the living/
family wing and garage on the left. The lot is
almost pie-shaped. This section of Sacramento
is quite flat (old riverbed land) and gets very
hot in the summer. The owners wanted a secluded,
green, forest-like effect for privacy but liked
the feeling of natural light and sunshine. There
was no existing planting.

HIGHLIGHTS:

Landscape architect Robert Acrea decided to tie
in with the circular theme of both the street and
the house. The inviting front yard/entry picks
this up with a grassy circle defined by concrete
aggregate walkway sections fanning out from the
circle. The driveway is brushed concrete.

In the backyard, the pool is angular and
asymetrical to contrast with the circular motif.
Shade is provided by two redwood decks with
trellising which run along the sides of the two
wings. The pool area is paved with concrete
aggregate. The living wing deck/trellis is
fenced with a double gate to protect small
children from the pool.

Another trellised area runs off at a right angle
from this wing to face the house from the
opposite side of the pool. Behind this trellis
is another double gate, using redwood supports
and wire fencing to keep an open feeling to the
yard.

Through the gate along more aggregate walkway
sections is a circular play area defined by
redwood headers and filled with redwood bark.
A circular redwood play deck is concentric to the
larger circle.

From the house, across the pool and to the left
of the large trellis is a grass-filled circle
which is used as a sunbathing area.

The greenhouse is off the left wing from the
pool and was ordered by the owner after the major
landscaping was done. The owner became so
interested in gardening that he took horticulture
courses and made the transition from a novice to
an experienced gardener after the house was
landscaped.

The owner specified plastic panes on the right
side of the greenhouse where it adjoins the
property line for privacy and plastic for the
roof to cut the extreme heat from the sun in this
area. The left and entrance are clear glass.
The greenhouse is used for potting and starting
plants and for refreshing house plants. The
redwood walkway and shelf-potting area were

FIGURE 3-4 CONT.

installed by the owner. The greenhouse features
a heater, cooler, humidifier, and fan to maintain
ideal climate conditions.

A redwood fence encloses the entire backyard.
Mulch cover is used as the major ground cover
to conserve water and limit upkeep. Trees and
shrubbery are low-lying to eventually fill in
the ground area. Bubbler sprinklers were
installed at the foot of each tree or growth
area to cut down on overall watering needs.

PLANTS SPECIFIED BY THE LANDSCAPE ARCHITECT:

Japanese Maple
European White Birch
St. John's Bread
Sweet Gum
Mayten Tree
Aleppo Pine
Carolina Cherry
Cork Oak
Chinese Tallow Tree
Coast Redwood
Chinese Elm
Lemon Bottle Brush
Hopseed Bush
Heavenly Bamboo
Mugho Pine
Tawhiwhi Kohuhu
Shiny Xylosma
Hahn's Ivy
Mexican Sedum
Star Jasmine
Dwarf Periwinkle

---

cost and sales price, if appropriate. Some editors also want
the brand names of all building materials and appliances used
in a building; most like to see the advertisements or sales
literature being used to sell units or lease space.

A week after you mail this material, call the editor to
check that your package has arrived. Ask if he or she needs
still more information. And don't hesitate to ask when you
will hear whether or not your project will be used in a story.
This is one way to avoid the awkward problem of an editor

SUBJECT: California Redwood Association Offices
                1 Lombard Street
                San Francisco, California 94111
                (415) 392-7880

ARCHITECTS: Environmental Planning and Research, Inc.
                649 Front Street
                San Francisco, California 94111
                (415) 433-4715
                Project Architect:
                  Joseph D. Chance, AIA (please credit)
                Contact:
                  Darryl T. Roberson, FAIA, President

FUNCTION: Headquarters of the trade association for the
                redwood industry, representing seven major
                redwood producers. The association develops and
                maintains markets for redwood products through
                nationwide promotion, including advertising,
                publicity, and the publishing of technical and
                design literature. The staff numbers eighteen
                persons. One office is occupied by the Redwood
                Inspection Service, an independent grading
                organization which sets and maintains standards
                for the industry.

                The space includes a total of 6,000 square feet.
                The spacious gallery/entry area is used for
                reception and entertainment functions and leads
                into the conference room. Office access is in a
                U-shaped floor plan. Other areas include a coffee
                room and a large mailing/printing/storage room.

HIGHLIGHTS: The building is a seventy-eight-year-old brick
                warehouse that was idle for many years until it
                was recently renovated as a developer/tenant
                project. A large architectural firm and the
                California Redwood Association were the first
                tenants, and there are now a total of six,
                including two architectural firms. The renova-
                tion is part of growing activity in this
                Embarcadero-bordered section of the city. Projects
                include just-completed Pier 39 and soon-to-get-
                underway Levi Square, world headquarters of Levi
                Strauss.

MATERIALS: The CRA offices were designed to showcase redwood
                lumber used as interior paneling and trim. Major
                elements are Clear All Heart tongue and groove
                redwood applied vertically and sapwood-streaked
                Clear grade shiplap used horizontally. In two
                areas, the entry and executive office, rippled
                redwood lumber in a specially milled Sculpturewood
                pattern by Forms and Surfaces in Santa Barbara
                has been used as a change of pace. All redwood
                surfaces are finished with two coats of Watco oil.

                The redwood contrasts with the textures of the
                original old brick walls. Massive, rugged Douglas

FIGURE 3-5 FACT SHEET, SAMPLE 2

35

FIGURE 3–5 CONT.

```
fir structural columns with original cast iron
capitals, new diagonal I-beams dictated by San
Francisco earthquake standards, huge exposed
wooden beams, and brightly painted heating/
cooling pipes are all dramatic design elements.

In the conference room is a unique beveled redwood
overhead ceiling inset with a lighting system.
A sliding wall of diagonal sapwood-streaked Clear
grade redwood opens to a second set of fabric-
covered display panels and a third layer giving
access to audio-visual facilities.  Glass doors
in the entry of the room support brass blinds
which echo brass detailing of the furniture.
Color accents of blue and rust are repeated
throughout the project in furniture, door
colors, office wall insets, and overhead fixtures.
Bright graphic prints and green plants complement
the design.

Furnishings -- Overall industrial carpet is Desert
Beige by Highland Court.  In the gallery, a
dramatic rust, blue, and beige inset carpet was
custom-made by Patrick Carpet Mills.  Blue
upholstered chairs are by Bennedetti.  The redwood
and brass coffee table was custom-made by Design
Workshop.  Conference room furnishings include a
custom-made densified redwood and brass table by
Design Workshop and blue velour and brass chairs
imported from Italy by Axiom Cesca.  The fabric is
Midnight Blue by Design Tex West.
```

PHOTOGRAPHER: Joshua Freiwald (no use fee necessary)

who holds your only original transparencies for three, six, or even nine months without giving you an idea when the project might be featured. If the editor is considering your project for a special issue, he or she will be able to tell you when the projects for that edition will be selected. If the editor doesn't mention a specific issue and only answers your question with a vague "Oh, I'll let you know," politely say that you will call again to check on the submittal on a specific date—perhaps six weeks from the date of your call. Remind the editor that you want your transparencies returned as soon as possible. This is especially important when your project or product is only newsworthy for a short period like a holiday season.

Often an editor will write a story from the material you provide in your first submittal. Sometimes he or she will call you and the others involved with a project for more information. At some magazines, the editors commission photography or photograph the sample products you send; at others, especially trade journals, editors expect you to provide the professional photography that will be used with a feature. If you are commissioning the photographer, ask the editor what size transparencies are needed. Most magazines use 35mm and 2¼-inch transparencies, but a few editors still insist on 4 × 5-inch transparencies. Consider the requirements of all the editors to whom you will send information on the project. If any of the magazines who are likely to feature the project require 4 × 5-inch transparencies, order these large transparencies now. The additional expense of 4 × 5 transparencies is less than the cost of having a project rephotographed.

If you have commissioned the photographer, he or she will deliver the transparencies and proof sheets to you. Study them carefully to determine which pictures show the features the editor is emphasizing in the story. From this group, select the pictures that also illustrate the points you want to make. Try not to send all the pictures to the same editor.

IF AN EDITOR HOLDS YOUR MATERIAL

If the editor tells you the editorial committee is meeting in four weeks and you have waited six weeks for a call or letter, telephone the editor or write a note like this:

> Needless to say, I'm anxious to know if my Pine Meadows project was selected for your issue on condominiums. Has the editorial committee made a decision yet?

> If you won't be able to include Pine Meadows in one of your future issues, I'd appreciate your returning my photographs as soon as possible.

If an editor holds your material for more than three months and does not respond to your reminder notes or your telephone calls, submit the story to another editor. (If you only had one set of color transparencies, send the second

---

Dear Mr. Diaz:

I just realized it's been four months since I sent you the
materials on our Pine Meadows condominiums. We discussed the
project briefly after you received the photographs, but at that
time you didn't know if you would be featuring the condos.   If
you will be using a story on Pine Meadows, would you give me a
call?

If you're not able to include the project in one of your upcoming
issues, would you return my photos in the envelope I've enclosed?
I'll need them when I send information on the project to other
editors early next month.

Sincerely,

John Jones

FIGURE 3-6   REMINDER LETTER, SAMPLE

editor one or two transparencies and a set of black-and-white
prints.) Notify the first editor that you're submitting your
material elsewhere with a note similar to the one in Figure
3-6. Send it by registered mail so you'll have proof it was
delivered.

Will you irritate editors by requesting that they return
your photographs? Perhaps. Most editors appreciate the
value of the material that you have sent them and realize that
they cannot hold it for months. There are some editors,
however, who want to keep packages of information in-
definitely, and they will be offended when you ask for a
definite publication date or your material. Your continued requests for your photographs may also embarrass the editor
who has lost your material.

WHEN YOU HAVE SUBMITTED TO ONE EDITOR
AND ANOTHER CALLS

Suppose you have submitted information on your firm to one
magazine, and, before you know whether it plans a story, the
editor of a competing magazine calls you for a story on the
same topic. What do you say? Something like this:

I'm glad to hear you're interested in our new merchandising training program. I'd like to tell you more about it, but another magazine is considering a story on the same program. May I call you back if the editors there decide not to run a story?

If you tell the second editor about the program without mentioning the first, both publications may run stories. You'll get a lot of publicity—once. Neither editor may speak to you again. If you tell the editor of the second magazine about the first's interest and he or she says, "Oh, that's all right, I'd still like the story," remember the editor at the first magazine. That editor will be dismayed to see a story on your firm in a competitor's magazine the same month—or worse, the month before—his or her own story is published.

SIMULTANEOUS SUBMITTALS

There are two situations in which it is appropriate to send information about the same project to more than one editor at the same time. The first occurs when you have news—for example, of a new factory or new product—that requires broad, immediate dissemination. For this announcement, issue a press release. The other situation occurs when you deal with magazines that do not compete with each other. Except in the unusual case where one editor will not feature a project that has appeared in any other publication, you can release the same information simultaneously to editors whose magazines are read by different groups of people. If you have opened a new ethnic restaurant, submit information on it to a regional magazine, a gourmet magazine and a travel magazine. If you are an interior designer who has just refurbished the interior of a hotel, send the story to an architectural or interiors journal, a hospitality industry magazine, and a travel columnist. So that you will have enough pictures of a project, ask the photographer for two or three original transparencies of each shot.

Once a story has been published, you are free to submit it to other journals. Editors of directly competing magazines like *Family Circle* and *Woman's Day, Popular Science* and *Popular Mechanics, Professional Builder* and *Builder* seldom feature the same project. However, editors of magazines whose readers are somewhat different, perhaps in age or geographic distribution, may be interested. Suggest a different editorial approach tailored to each magazine's audience. For example, a few years ago, lemon growers used recipes to promote lemons in women's magazines; in fashion magazines they emphasized how lemons could be used as a beauty aid.

Tell editors which other publications have printed or scheduled features on a project. Sometimes the easiest way to do this is by sending copies of earlier articles, especially those from publications with very different audiences. If you're sending information about a custom house to *Sunset*, include the *San Francisco Chronicle* article on the project. If you're sending pictures of your new restaurant to *Restaurant Hospitality*, send a photocopy of the *New York Times* review.

HOW YOUR PROJECT MAY BE FEATURED

Will your project be the cover story? The topic of a four-page spread? Or will it receive only a few lines in a long roundup story? If you have studied a publication carefully and you know what its regular features are, you have some idea of how much space your project or product will receive. For example, if you are submitting details on your firm's new models for a magazine's annual story about boats, expect only a paragraph or two. When you submit news of a new building product to *Architectural Record* or *Builder,* the magazine may run a small picture and a few lines of information.

Let's suppose you've studied the editorial calendar and read enough back issues to know that a magazine will soon feature products like yours. To determine how appropriate your products are for this issue, call the editor before you send any material. After you have sent the material and called to check that it has arrived, ask the editor if he or she knows how your information may be used. Editors don't like publicity hogs, but they understand that you want the best exposure possible. They also may know whether the longer features wrapped around color photographs are read as carefully as the short stories published with black-and-white pictures in the front of the magazine.

USING PUBLICITY IN MARKETING

How do firms use publicity in their marketing programs? At Bear Essentials, Marilyn Wenker used her publicity in *Ms.* to motivate her sales representatives, and she quoted the story in her sales letter to retailers who did not yet carry her line. At Lah-ti-dah, Rinna Wolfe sent copies of a Berkeley, California, *Gazette* story about her first paper doll with the press release on the second doll. At Wudtke Watson Davis, Inc., Ruth Kirk sent copies of magazine features with brochures when the architectural firm mailed information to potential clients. Like many other design firms, Wudtke Watson Davis also inserted reprints in brochures for client presentations. Reprints can also be used as part of a regular direct mail program to potential and current clients.

There is something almost magical about publicity; overnight it seems to give you more credibility with people. Whether they ever see the original story, whether they've ever heard of the magazine, people are impressed that an editor found your firm important enough to publicize. That's why being published is worth far more than the exposure you get in the one issue of a magazine. Besides being more impressive than a brochure or sales catalog you write and print yourself, reprints of a story can be less expensive. Five hundred copies of a four-page color story about your firm may cost $1,000, but that's substantially less than you would pay a printer to set the type, make the color separations, and print a folder. The magazine also does the writing and the page design for you.

Reprints

Many magazines will sell you reprints of the stories that have been published about you. A few other publications will lend you the color separations and copy and allow you to have reprints made by your own printer. Reprints must be ordered early, usually when the magazine is being printed. When your story has been accepted for publication, ask the editor how you can order reprints. The cost of reprints depends on the quality of paper used, the number of pages to be reprinted, the number of reprints ordered, and whether the story has black-and-white or color photography. For example, 500 copies (the minimum order) of a two-page color reprint from *Builder* cost $900 in 1980; 1,000 copies of a four-page color reprint cost $1,100. The reprints are printed on 70-pound stock instead of the 40-pound paper used in the magazine; they can be ordered with the cover of the magazine issue in which your story appeared.

Photocopying the Original Story

Photocopying any part of a copyrighted story or magazine without the publisher's permission is illegal. If you want to make a few copies of a story about your firm or your industry, write the publisher, specifiying how you will use the photo-copies and how many copies you will make.

Use Extra Copies of the Magazine

When you know you'll only need a few copies of a feature, you'll save money by ordering extra copies of the magazine. Even at $5 a copy, twenty-five or fifty copies of a trade journal will be less expensive than the minimum order of reprints. And you may be able to reduce the cost per copy with a bulk rate; ask the editor if the magazine has special rates for quantity sales. You can use the entire magazine; send copies to your sales representatives, your dealers, and a select group of clients. Display the magazine in your office, too. If you would prefer to use just the pages with your feature, use a single-edge razor blade or a utility knife like an X-acto to slit the spine of the magazine and remove your story. Staple the pages to the magazine cover for display or distribution.

OFFICE DISPLAYS

Your office is one of the first examples of your work that your potential customers see. A well-designed office will say more about your philosophy and your attention to detail and budget than any brochure you can print or any advertisement you can buy. By displaying copies of the articles that have been written about you in your office, you will show visitors the variety of work that you have done. For more ideas on what to display and how it can be presented, see Chapter 12.

4

TRADE ASSOCIATION AND MANUFACTURER PUBLICITY

From Chapter 3 you know that popular magazines and newspapers are not your only sources of publicity. Many firms and trade associations publish magazines, brochures, and advertisements. Some have publicity writers who develop articles for company publications. Many of these stories are sent to magazines and wire services. And, as Chapter 7 points out, publicity writers often pay for the professional photography of projects they feature.

This chapter, intended primarily for those in design and construction, will introduce you to corporate and association publications. You will find examples of the newsletters, advertisements, and sales literature many firms publish. You will also find case histories that describe what can happen when a publicist promotes your projects.

PUBLICATIONS

Redwood News is one of the many publications issued by trade associations. Usually eight pages, this magazine-style booklet is published three times a year. Its black-and-white pictures feature residential, commercial, and garden structures built with redwood. Published by the California Redwood Association, *Redwood News* is sent to 42,000 architects, builders, engineers, interior designers, landscape architects, and lumber wholesalers in the United States and in several foreign countries.

Mallet & Froe, published by the Red Cedar Shingle & Handsplit Shake Bureau, is a quarterly that's sent to 22,000 architects, contractors, roofing contractors, lumber dealers, and editors in the United States, Canada, and Australia. It runs black-and-white pictures of residential, commercial, remodeling, and vacation home projects.

Newsline, a bimonthly publication of the Simpson Timber Company, is sent to some 2,000 editors and lumber dealers and distributors in the United States. In the four to eight pages of each issue, *Newsline* features projects built with Simpson products. *Simpson,* the company's bimonthly employee magazine, also pictures projects built with the company's products.

There are many other publications that might feature your products. For their names, talk to the sales representatives who call on you and the dealers from whom you order materials. Don't forget people like your banker and your accountant; their marketing departments probably produce glossy internal magazines about their services and their customers.

ADVERTISEMENTS AND CATALOGS

Many of these firms and associations also use photographs and case studies of outstanding buildings in their advertisements and product catalogs. For example, each year the California Redwood Association features as many as thirty new projects in advertisements and catalogs like *Decks Do It, Renew It with Redwood, Redwood Homes*, and *Interior-Exterior Guide*. The Red Cedar Shingle & Handsplit Shake Bureau usually pictures ten projects in ads and as many as fifteen in product catalogs. Simpson Timber may feature as many as fifty new projects in product catalogs and inserts for building industry catalogs like *Sweet's Catalog File* and *The WoodBook*. Other projects are featured in the new ads Simpson prepares each year.

If you use skylights, send information on your projects to Naturalite; if you use built-up roofs, send a description of your project to the Johns-Manville advertising manager for building systems. If you use site-cast reinforced concrete, write the Concrete Reinforcing Steel Institute. If you use Olympic Stain, write its advertising and public relations agency.

What other companies feature projects in their ads? Read trade and consumer magazines carefully; you'll see pictures of projects in ads for paint, plumbing equipment, and prefinished siding; for paving material, plywood and planking; for steel, stone, and shingles. When you see an ad that shows a project and credits the architect and builder, jot down the manufacturer's name. Write the marketing director or advertising manager to ask how you should submit photographs and information on the projects you've designed or built with the firm's products.

Credit Lines

Some publications, ads, and product catalogs do not include credit lines for the architects and builders of the projects featured. Before you submit material to a publicist, determine the firm or association's policy on credits. Ask the publicist or advertising manager for a credit line on pictures of your work—but remember that a credit line is only one of the benefits of having your work published in an ad or catalog. The publicist may pay for the photography of your project and make the pictures available to you at little or no cost; you may receive free copies of the publication to distribute with your brochure.

WHAT A PRODUCT PUBLICIST CAN DO

What can happen when a product publicist learns of your work? You may find your project mentioned on the back page of a product catalog—or splashed across the cover of a trade journal. Your work may be described in a press release sent to a local newspaper for its annual home improvement issue—or it may be pictured in an advertisement that appears year after year in professional, trade, and general interest magazines.

Publicists don't produce stories or publications on every good project they see. Like an editor, a publicist often has very specific needs and a limited budget; he or she can photograph and feature only a few of the many projects submitted each year. Often, the type of project and the materials a publicist can promote are dictated by corporate policy.

Many features result from calls to sales representatives or technical advisers. For example, when an Iowa builder called the American Plywood Association field representative for advice on using treated plywood as a foundation, the builder's name was turned in to an association publicist. She interviewed the builder on her next trip to the Midwest, used his comments in several general press releases on the wood foundation—and sent her notes to the association's advertising agency. A few months later, the builder's picture and comments were published in a two-page advertisement on wood foundations that appeared in several issues of architectural and building journals.

An Oregon builder who called the association for help found himself in print, too. When visiting the builder at his home office on an Appaloosa horse ranch, the association representative discovered that the builder's wife and sons were raising thousands of earthworms in plywood bins full of horse manure and water. The details went to the association headquarters, where the story appeared in a newsletter sent to executives of plywood manufacturing firms. After a publicist had the builder and his wife photographed, the story appeared in several national agricultural magazines, including the publication for Appaloosa owners.

When a San Francisco bay area builder called the California Redwood Association for advice on redwood grades, he met both the technical adviser and a publicist. Months later, his projects were featured in a seven-page *Housing* story and in the *House Beautiful Remodeling Manual*. Then the association helped him design and finance a remodeling project in his Victorian house; that project has since been published in several California Redwood publications and in consumer magazines.

A Marin County builder didn't even have to call the Redwood Association to get his custom homes on the cover of *Professional Builder*. The redwood publicists, who were visiting Marin County to photograph a project next door, called him. Besides the *Professional Builder* story, the project has been featured in two California Redwood publications. The architect who designs the builder's projects has benefited, too; he has had other examples of his work published in Redwood Association literature.

HOW TO SUBMIT MATERIAL TO PUBLICISTS

Send publicists information on the projects in the same way Chapter 3 suggests submitting material to magazine editors. First, try to determine what material the publicist needs; read the company's existing publications and talk to a sales representative or the publicist. Then obtain the product specifications. If you're sending information on a custom house sided with redwood to the editor of *Redwood News*,

you will need to know the board size and grade. When you
send the American Plywood Association information on a
roof deck, mention the plywood thickness and grade and the
joist size and spacing. When you're calling Johns-Manville,
have a list of every J-M product you've used in the building.

By providing this much detail, you assure the publicist
that his or her product is indeed on your project. (In pictures,
hardboard siding panels can be mistaken for plywood siding
and cedar boards can be confused with redwood.) More important, you're providing information that will help a publicist
decide whether to promote your building. The publicist
may be revising a catalog on institutional buildings with
built-up roofs when your construction pictures of a church arrive; he or she may be planning a story on pressure
preservative-treated wood when he or she receives your note
about a wood foundation.

What is better—writing or calling? If you don't have the
name of a specific publicist, try a note. If you telephone, your
call may be transferred from one department to another. This
is expensive and frustrating. If the publication or advertisement in which you're interested is produced by an advertising or public relations agency, you may have difficulty finding someone who knows the best contact at the agency. (If
you know that a firm or an association staff is small, you
probably can reach the publicist you want by asking the
switchboard operator for "the person who edits *Redwood
News*" or "the person who produces your sales literature on
heat pumps.")

There are two other important reasons for writing.
Publicists want projects that look good, and on the phone it's
hard to describe your project. In this case, a picture is worth
10,000 words. Many publicity departments also practice decision by committee; several members of the staff will review
pictures and details of a project before it's considered for use.

When you send the first package of information to a
publicist, include the material listed in Chapter 3. Write a letter describing the project and your work; point out how often
you use the manufacturer's products. Send well-focused

Organization	Publications	Contact	Send	Notes
California Redwood Association	Redwood News Advertisements Product catalogs	California Redwood Association 1 Lombard Street San Francisco, California 94111	Color slides that show entire project and details; fact sheet	Submits materials to trade journals and consumer magazines; sometimes pays for photography.
Red Cedar Shingle & Handsplit Shake Bureau	Mallet & Froe Advertisements Product catalogs	Franklin C. Welch Advertising Manager Shake Bureau Suite 275 515 116th Avenue, Northeast Bellevue, Washington 98004	Photographs; fact sheet; statement on project and use of shakes or shingles (not endorsement)	Submits materials to trade journals and consumer magazines; sometimes pays for photography.
American Plywood Association	Advertisements Product catalogs	Information Services American Plywood Association P.O. Box 11700 Tacoma, Washington 98411	Photographs; fact sheet	Submits materials to trade journals and consumer magazines; sometimes pays for photography.
Simpson Timber Company	Newsline Simpson	Relta Gray Associates 1011 Lloyd Bldg. Seattle, Washington 98101	Color slides; fact sheet; product specifications; plans	Relta Gray Associates does all product publicity and submits material to trade journals.

	Advertisements Product catalogs	Dean Matthews Advertising and Promotion Manager Simpson Timber Co. 1011 Lloyd Bldg. Seattle, Washington 98101	
Olympic Stain	Advertisements Product catalogs	Kraft Smith, Inc. 200 1st West Seattle, Washington 98109	Slides; description of project; statement on use of stain	Submits material to trade journals; sometimes pays for photography.
Naturalite, Inc.	Advertisements Product catalogs	Advertising Manager Naturalite, Inc. Box 28636 Dallas, Texas 75228		
Johns-Manville	Advertisements Product catalogs Newsletters	Johns-Manville Ken-Caryl Ranch Denver, Colorado 80217	Photography; information on every part of building using J-M products	Public relations agency submits material to trade journals; will pay for construction and finish photography.
Concrete Reinforcing Steel Institute	Advertisements	Vice President Marketing and Promotion CRSI 180 North LaSalle Street Chicago, Illinois 60601		Submits materials to trade journals.

FIGURE 4-1 TRADE ASSOCIATIONS AND MANUFACTURERS THAT PROMOTE PROJECTS

Editor, <u>Redwood News</u>
California Redwood Association
1 Lombard Street
San Francisco, California 94111

Here's a few photographs and some information on a ski cabin I
hope you'll be able to feature in <u>Redwood News</u>.

Constructed near Lake Tahoe, the cabin is sided with rough-sawn
redwood plywood. Joints are detailed with 1 x 6 boards. The
living room is paneled with 1 x 6 All Heart redwood. Scheduled
to be completed within the next month, the cabin has 1,500 square
feet of living space on the main and loft levels. It's one of
three I've built this summer in the same recreational home
development. The cost was approximately $100 per square foot,
including a sauna and a 14 x 16-foot deck of 2 x 6 Garden grade
redwood.

Sincerely,

Joe Brown

Enclosures: Three 35mm slides of exterior, one of living room
             floor plan

FIGURE 4-2   COVER LETTER TO PUBLICIST, SAMPLE

black-and-white prints or color slides. Avoid pictures taken
with an instant-loading or self-developing camera; they won't
show the details a publicist needs to see. Send floor and site
plans, too; if you haven't redrawn the plans on $8 \frac{1}{2} \times 11$-inch
sheets, send only the blueprints that show the main floor plan
and the site. Publicists don't have room in their offices or on
their desks for every page of a set of working drawings.
Describe any problems with the site, the construction
methods, or the merchandising program; include a drawing of
any unusual construction details. The fact sheet you send
(see Figures 3-4 and 3-5 for examples) should also list the
construction materials and their applications, the construction cost, and sales price.

Tell the publicist whether you've submitted information
on the project to editors or to other publicists. Because a
publicist may be thinking of particular magazines when he or
she agrees to publicize your project, it is important that he or

she know which editors have told you they cannot use the project. To help a publicist, mention what news angles you've pointed out to the editors you've approached. After reviewing the information on your project, the publicist may see several different reasons why editors may be interested in the project.

When you find that a publicist cannot use a story on your project, ask him or her to recommend other publicists who may be interested in it. One publicist may not know exactly what other firms and trade associations need, but can provide valuable names of people and organizations.

5

THE PRESS RELEASE

What is a press release? It's news—about you. It's the short story about your new firm, your new partner, a design award, a new product. A press release is an effective means of getting information to the news media. Often, you will find that press releases are written for you by others. When you receive an award, for example, the program sponsors release the news; when you receive a major commission, your client usually issues the release. There are, however, many appropriate occasions for you to issue press releases; learning how to produce them will give you an important public relations skill. There's no mystique to press releases; they are easy and economical to write, print, and mail.

When should you write a press release? How should the facts be organized? This chapter will answer these questions and provide information on different reproduction methods, the media that should receive your release, and the kind of publicity you can expect.

WRITING THE PRESS RELEASE

When do you write a press release? When you're ready to announce something, usually a single event, that will be of interest to people outside your office. For example, issue a press release when you establish a new firm, hire an associate, add a partner, promote an employee, or move to a new office.

To write a release, you will need the basics: the same "who," "what," "why," "where," "when," and "how" you remember from high school journalism. You already have most of this; it's on the fact sheets that you've prepared on projects, it's in your general files, or it's jotted down on the notes that cover your desk. To gather accurate information about the people with whom you work, use a questionnaire like Figure 5-1. Ask all new employees to complete it on their first day on the job; then, once a year, ask the people on your staff to update the material.

In organizing the release, start with the information that's most important to your reader and work down to the least important. Use simple, fairly short sentences and nontechnical language; double check the spelling of every name and the accuracy of every fact, especially firm names and addresses, people's titles, and cost and square footage figures.

When do you issue your first press release? Ideally, when you open your business. All you need are those basic facts about you, including your new firm's name and address, your products and services, your partners and associates, and

Complete and return to the Public Relations Department.

Full name _____ Nickname _____

Home address _____

Business address _____

_____ Phone _____

Present job title _____

Brief summary of responsibilities _____

_____

To whom do you report? _____

Operation/Division _____

Location _____

Date of original employment with us _____

Other positions you've held with us:

Position	Operation	Dates
_____	_____	_____
_____	_____	_____
_____	_____	_____
_____	_____	_____

Positions you've held with other employers:

Position	Company	Dates
_____	_____	_____
_____	_____	_____
_____	_____	_____
_____	_____	_____

Professional associations to which you belong:

_____

_____

_____

_____

FIGURE 5-1 PERSONAL HISTORY QUESTIONNAIRE

60

FIGURE 5-1 CONT.

Education:

Institution	Degree Conferred	Graduation Date
_____	_____	_____
_____	_____	_____
_____	_____	_____

Date of birth _____ Birthplace _____

If married, spouse's name _____

Names of children _____

_____

I'd like press releases written about me sent to these publications
(include alumni paper and hometown paper if desired):

Name	Address
_____	_____
_____	_____
_____	_____
_____	_____

I authorize the Public Relations staff to use this information in producing press releases.

_____
Signature

_____
Date

your experience and education. Start with the most newsworthy information: the fact that you're opening an office.

Headline: BLAKE JONES OPENS
FLORIST'S SHOP

First (Lead) Paragraph: Blake Jones has established Petal
Power, a florist's shop, at 105 West
Main Street, Auburn.

Although editors seldom use the same headline, it
quickly tells them who's doing what: Jones is opening a
florist shop. The first paragraph repeats this and provides important additional information: the name and address of the
firm. Editors of national magazines and large newspapers
probably will not have the space for more information than
this, but smaller publications may want to know about your
education and experience. Your experience is more recent and
thus is more newsworthy, so it is first in this sample:

Jones, who formerly was with Seattle florist H. B. James as
assistant manager, is a 1978 graduate of Washington State
University.

If you send the release to your hometown newspaper, add
a paragraph about where you're from:

A native of Davenport, Lincoln County, Jones is the son of
Judge and Mrs. Bentley Jones of Davenport.

Use the same format for more complicated stories, too.
For example, if you are reporting that you've promoted
several employees, you might say:

Headline: TUKWILA TOYMAKERS PROMOTES BROWN,
COLLINS, SMITH

Lead: Three members of the Tukwila Toymakers, Inc.
sales staff have been promoted.

Jo Brown has been named western division sales manager, and Cary Collins and Bob Smith have been promoted to assistant sales managers at headquarters.

Here the first few words again tell editors "who" and "what": Brown, Collins, and Smith have all been promoted at Tukwila Toymakers. The first paragraph provides a quick summary of the news; the details on the individuals promoted and their new jobs come in the second paragraph. The next three paragraphs provide the most important information about each one of the people promoted:

Brown, formerly assistant sales manager for the western division, joined Tukwila Toymakers in 1979. A graduate of the University of Washington, she previously worked for Frederick & Nelson as a buyer.

Collins joined the company as an accountant in 1978 and was named a sales representative in 1980. He is a graduate of Seattle Pacific University.

Smith, who has worked as a sales representative in the Midwest since joining the toymaker in 1979, graduated from the University of Iowa.

Brown has been listed first because, of the three, she holds the most important position within the company; this makes her promotion the most newsworthy. Because Collins and Smith have been promoted to positions of equal importance to the company and the Tukwila area readers, they are listed in alphabetical order. Figure 5-3 shows you how this release might be rewritten for Smith's hometown newspaper.

If you need to convey more information about each person, use another series of short paragraphs:

Brown, a Renton resident, is a member of the Tukwila Chamber of Commerce and Seattle Women in Business.

Collins lives in Burien, where he is active in Kiwanis and the Lions Club. He is also a member of the SPU Alumni Association.

Smith, who lives in Tukwila, is pursuing an MBA at the University of Puget Sound. A former semipro baseball player, he coaches the Tukwila Little League teams.

The release concludes with a paragraph of general information about the firm that might be included in every release:

Established in 1965, Tukwila Toymakers, Inc. employs sixty-five people at its Tukwila headquarters and in sales offices in Trenton, New Jersey; Lubbock, Texas; and Des Moines, Iowa.

Once you've written a headline and the story, you only need a few more elements for the finished release. If your firm name, address, and telephone number (including area code) are not already on the letterhead, add them and the name of someone (probably you) editors can contact for more information. The final requirement: the release "date."

In theory, the release date indicates when an editor is free to publish the story; this, however, is only theory. Send out a press release only when you're willing to have the information published. Instead of an actual date, most press releases have phrases like "For release: Immediately" or "For immediate release." Under this add the date the release was mailed. This tells the editor when a release was issued; it will also help you in filing.

As you'll see in Figure 5-2, the name of the contact should go in the upper right corner, and the release date and date mailed in the upper left. The release should start about a third of the page down from the headline. Skip a couple of spaces after the headline and then start typing the release; double space, using wide (about 1½-inch) margins.

Whenever a release exceeds a page, end the first page with a completed paragraph and the word "more" centered in parentheses at the bottom of the page. A few spaces below the last line of the release, type the word "end" or the symbols "###" or "-30-." Staple the two pages together in the upper left corner. Never staple the release to photographs, renderings, or other materials.

PETAL POWER: 105 West Main Street, Auburn, Washington 98000
               (206) 833-0000

                                        CONTACT: Blake Jones

FOR RELEASE: Immediately

DATE MAILED: May 1, 1981

          BLAKE JONES ESTABLISHES PETAL POWER

     Blake Jones has established Petal Power, a florist's shop,
at 105 West Main Street, Auburn.

     Jones, who formerly was with Seattle florist H. B. James
as assistant manager, is a 1978 graduate of Washington State
University.

     A native of Davenport, Lincoln County, Jones is the son of
Judge and Mrs. Bentley Jones, Davenport.

                              ###

FIGURE 5-2   PRESS RELEASE, SAMPLE 1

TUKWILA TOYMAKERS, INC.   P.O. Box 336
                               Tukwila, Washington 98000
                               (206) 999-0000

                               CONTACT: Red Nelson, president

FOR RELEASE: Immediately

DATE MAILED: May 1, 1981

          BOB SMITH PROMOTED AT TUKWILA TOYMAKERS

     Altoona resident Bob Smith has been promoted to assistant
sales manager at Tukwila Toymakers, Inc.

     Smith has been transferred to the firm's Tukwila,
Washington, headquarters from the Des Moines sales office,
where he has worked as a sales representative since joining
the toymaker in 1979.

     Two other members of the Tukwila Toymakers, Inc. sales
staff have also been promoted. Jo Brown has been named
western division sales manager and Cary Collins has been
named assistant sales manager at headquarters. Both are
Tukwila area residents.
                              END

FIGURE 5-3   PRESS RELEASE, SAMPLE 2

65

PRODUCING THE RELEASE

How do you produce the release? You or your secretary can type each copy; if you're issuing only a handful, that's an economical solution. If you will be mailing out more than a dozen releases, have the original photocopied. This is a particularly economical and attractive alternative if you have or can use (perhaps at a copy shop) a sheet-fed, plain-paper copy machine with which you can use your own letterhead. Don't photocopy releases if you must use one of the inexpensive machines that operates with off-color, coated paper. The press releases will be unattractive and hard to read. Editors who mark instructions to printers on stories will have difficulty writing on the coated paper.

For twenty-five or more copies, check with a "quick copy" or "instant" print shop. For about $5 you can have fifty clean, sharp reproductions of the release. Some shops print while you wait. Others take only a few hours. If your press release is more than one page long, have each page printed on a separate sheet. A press release printed on both sides of a sheet of paper is almost impossible to edit.

Whether you photocopy the release or have it printed on an offset press, you must provide the original. For the best possible reproduction, type the original with a carbon film ribbon or a new nylon ribbon. Use a machine that doesn't skip or jump. Use good quality opaque white paper, even if your stationery is not white. If the release will be copied onto your letterhead, use plain paper for the original. If you are a poor typist or have an undependable typewriter, check your local newspaper's classified advertisements or the Yellow Pages for typing services. Many résumé writing and printing services also do typing. Typists usually charge $1 to $2 per page.

WHAT DO YOU SEND WITH THE RELEASE?

Once you've decided how to prepare the release, consider whether or not you should send any other information with it. For example, should you send a photograph of yourself with the release announcing your new firm? Probably not, unless you know that the newspapers and magazines in your area use such pictures. Generally, large newspapers and national magazines do not print photographs with routine announcements.

When you do send photographs of individuals, the pictures should be very recent photographs that have been posed so they can be cropped and reduced to small "head" or "mug" shots. The prints should be sharp black-and-white glossies with the individual's name lightly penciled on the back. Prints need not be large; the cost of an 8 × 10-inch print and the postage to mail it are unnecessary expenses. But avoid the very small prints sometimes offered in discount packages. Never submit a self-developing (for example, Polaroid) photograph to any publication.

If you're announcing the construction or remodeling of a building, you will want to send out photographs of the model or copies of the rendering. Any models built to be photographed should be carefully crafted to resemble real buildings; they should be photographed on a plain, preferably seamless, background. Because the photographs may be published across several columns in a newspaper, prints should be 5 × 7 inches or larger.

Copies of renderings are less expensive to produce and more likely to be printed. If you're planning to reproduce a rendering, draw it in black ink on white paper. Apply color to an overlay that can be removed for reproduction. For renderings in the 8 × 10-inch size you will want for mailing to publications, reduce the images by having them photostatted or by photographing them in black and white. The photostat or photograph probably can be reproduced by the same copy shop that prints your releases. For the best possible reproduction, have the copy shop use black ink and a heavy, opaque white paper. Photocopies of renderings will not have enough contrast to reproduce well in newspapers.

Put your name or the project name on a label on the back of the rendering if this information doesn't appear on the front. Package it between sheets of cardboard in an oversize envelope to prevent wrinkling. Mark "Do Not Fold" clearly on the envelope.

If the subject of a rendering or a photograph is clearly identified, a caption is not necessary. However, whenever you send out photographs of a group (for example, at a ground breaking ceremony), include captions that at least identify the individuals shown.

> Breaking ground for the new florist shop, Petal Power, at 105 West Main Street, Auburn, are, from left, Bob Smith, contractor; Blake Jones, Petal Power owner, and Mike Murphy, loan officer, First National Bank.

Should you send a cover letter with the release? Yes, if you have additional information that is not important to the story, but may be of interest to one publication's readers. For example, if Jones is sending a press release on his new firm to his college alumni paper, he will include a letter describing his current alumni association activities.

> Dear Editor:
>
> I'm pleased to announce that I'm opening my own shop after several years with a Seattle firm. I'll continue to be active in the King County Cougar Club. I've served as treasurer this year and will be taking over as vice president in the fall.
>
> If you'd like any additional information, don't hesitate to call or write me.

Most press releases are printed, but often on a space available basis. Whether or not you advertise in a publication will not influence a reputable editor's decision to use a press release about your firm. Someday, however, you may meet an editor who expects you to buy an ad before your press release is printed. There are even a few editors who return press releases with advertising rate cards.

When you submit a press release to a publication, never ask the editor to send you a copy of the issue in which the story appears; if you want to know if a magazine or newspaper publishes your release, read the publication regularly or engage a clipping bureau to read it for you. You can read out-of-town newspapers and trade journals at many local libraries. To obtain a copy of the issue with a story about you, write the publication, specifying the issue you want and enclosing the appropriate payment.

Routine press releases and cover letters like the example should be directed to the editor. When you write to a daily newspaper, address your release to the most appropriate department editor, at least by title. For example, the story about your new firm should be sent to the business editor. Send only one copy of each release to each publication. Releases sent to broadcast stations should be addressed to the news director.

SENDING OUT THE RELEASE

Now, which media should receive your press release? The local daily and weekly newspapers and perhaps the local radio and television stations are obvious choices. Then there's the regional and national architectural press. Remember club and professional organization newsletters, college alumni newspapers, and hometown newspapers.

To show you what a new design firm's mailing list might include, let's look again at Blake Jones and Petal Power. Because this hypothetical firm is located in Auburn, Jones will send a release to the *Auburn Globe-News*, the local paper. Auburn is between Seattle and Tacoma, and Jones has worked in Seattle with people whom he hopes to attract to his new shop, so he will also send a release to the business editors at the *Seattle Times* and the *Seattle Post-Intelligencer*, the city's two daily papers, and to the *Journal of Commerce* and the *Seattle Business Journal*, the business papers. Because many Auburn residents also read the Tacoma paper, Jones will send a release to the *Tacoma News Tribune*, the one Tacoma daily.

Other releases will go to the *Davenport Times*, the weekly paper published in the community where Jones grew up and his parents still live, and to the monthly *Hilltopics*, his college alumni paper.

Jones doesn't belong to any professional groups yet, but he will send releases to the news editors of national and regional floral and nursery trade journals.

Once you've listed the media that should receive your release, you will need their addresses and perhaps the names of their editors and news directors. To compile this information, first check the newspapers and magazines you read regularly; you will find the address of each editorial office in the masthead, a block of type on one of the first pages. (Magazines often publish the mastheads on their contents pages.)

For the names and addresses of other newspapers in your area, check the Yellow Pages. Not all of the papers listed are interested in general news; when you read the listings carefully, you will see that many of the papers are published for specific groups. Some are interested in a specific neighborhood; others are trade papers.

If you would like to send a release to papers outside your community, there are several directories that list newspaper names and addresses. The least expensive (sometimes free) and often most accurate lists are available from regional or state newspaper associations. Sometimes these are called press or newspaper publishers' associations, and they are often listed under "newspaper" in the Yellow Pages of major cities. Or you can write the National Newspaper Association, which sells a list of the associations, the addresses of their headquarters, and the names of their managers.

For more details, consult one of the many national directories listed in Appendix A. Most of these are revised annually and include information on daily and weekly newspapers; many also list trade and consumer magazines. Sold for $35 or more, the directories are often available in libraries, usually at the reserve desk.

COST VERSUS RETURN

What does it cost to produce a press release and what kind of return can you expect? Once again, let's suppose you're

Blake Jones. You spend a couple of hours writing the release and making out the mailing list. To get the releases you need for mailing and a few extra copies for filing, you have your part-time secretary type an original; this is copied on your own letterhead at the local copy shop. The only other expense is postage. Excluding time and ordinary office supplies, you've spent about $5.

What can you expect for this expenditure? You will probably be mentioned in the regional and national magazines' columns on new firms; the Seattle and Tacoma papers will run the news in their "people in business" columns or in short news stories on the business or real estate pages. Your alumni and hometown papers may publish short stories based on your press release, or they may include the news in columns like "Class News" or "Local Items." The most thorough coverage probably will come in the Auburn paper; the editor may send out a reporter to interview the new local businessman.

Measuring the value of this publicity in dollars and cents is difficult. As you will remember from the case histories mentioned in earlier chapters, press coverage sometimes causes an immediate increase in your business. More often, the benefits take longer to be recognized and they cannot be attributed to specific press releases or feature stories. Sometimes the only immediate return on your investment of effort and money is the personal satisfaction of seeing your firm recognized in the press.

Let's say your objective in issuing this first press release is awareness; you simply want as many people as possible to know you've established your own office. How well have you succeeded?

Besides announcing that you're in business, this release may help you get to know the other business people in town and the media. Business people may remember your name when they meet you at professional, civic, and social activities; your former classmates and neighbors may mention your name to their friends in the Auburn area; and the local reporters may think of you when they research stories on young businessmen.

Release Title	Date Mailed	Distribution	Use
Blake Jones opens florist shop	May 1	Seattle Times	May 3, 1-inch story
		Seattle P-I	May 3, business column
		Daily Journal of Commerce	May 3, 2-inch story
		Seattle Business Journal	
		Tacoma News Tribune	May 5, business column
		Auburn Globe-News	May 4, 8-inch feature with photo
		Davenport Times	May 11, 2-inch story
		WSU Hilltopics	September issue, "Tracking the Cougars"

FIGURE 5-4 PRESS RELEASE, LOG

FILING

By filing copies of your press releases, you'll maintain a record of what information has been released to the media. You'll also create a valuable reference for yourself. By checking the release file, you can quickly tell when people were hired, when projects were started, and when products were introduced.

Your press release file also makes writing new releases easier. When you're writing a story about the employees you've promoted, use the last story on promotions for a guide. Reuse the information in press releases. For example, for that story on promotions, use some of the paragraphs from the press releases you wrote when you hired these people.

To file releases, add a file folder marked "press releases" to your general office file. Staple a copy of your mailing list for each release to one of the extra copies. Add clippings to the file as you receive them. Or set aside a file drawer for press releases and file each release and the clippings of it in a separate folder. If you prefer to file your releases and mailing lists in a three-ring binder, keep the clippings in transparent plastic sleeves. Use dividers to separate the releases by topic or year of issue. To record which publications use your press releases, set up a log like Figure 5-4. List the releases by headline and date, the publications, and the dates when the stories are published.

6

WHEN A SINGLE PRESS RELEASE DOESN'T TELL THE STORY

Sometimes you can't tell the whole story in a single press release or even in one lengthy feature. If you're organizing a charity auction, opening a branch bank, or building a model home, you will want a well-coordinated series of press releases and a press conference. You may also want a tour or an open house for the public.

Intended for people in nonprofit organizations as well as for people in business, this chapter tells you how to plan a complete publicity program. You'll find suggestions for press releases, feature stories, press kits, and publicity photographs; schedules for open houses and press conferences; and a detailed list of what to consider when you're planning a tour of your facility.

PRESS RELEASES

A series of press releases allows you to introduce your project to the press and the public with a short story. Then, as additional information becomes available, you can present it in other releases. For example, in your first press release about a charity auction, mention the group planning the auction, the organizers, the purpose of the auction, and the auction date. In the second story, list the committee members and describe the auction theme and the first donations. For the third release, write a feature story about some of the unusual contributions to the auction.

If you're handling the publicity on a bank's new branch office, start your series of press releases by announcing the neighborhood or town where a new branch is planned. In your second story, announce that banking authorities have approved the branch and that a site has been selected. Follow this with a description and a rendering of the planned building and the names of the architects, landscape architects, and contractors who have been hired. In the fourth press release, report on the construction and give the projected completion date; for the fifth release, send a photograph and brief biographical sketch of the new branch manager. Later, describe the other staff members and the services and facilities the branch will offer; in your final story before the branch opens, tell about the grand opening festivities that are planned and list the bank, banking authority, and local officials who will participate in the opening ceremony.

To attract the local photographers, plan a colorful grand opening. Fly the branch manager in by balloon to officially

77

unlock the doors; use a six-foot-long pair of scissors to cut the traditional ribbon; or recognize the neighborhood's ethnic character with old country music, dancing, refreshments, and costumes. If the local newspapers do not send photographers to the ribbon-cutting ceremony, photograph that and any other newsworthy opening activities. Have the pictures processed immediately and delivered to the papers in time for their next editions. Newspapers with small staffs often use pictures like these. You will also want to give the newspapers a story on the number of accounts opened, the total dollars deposited, and the door prize winners.

Keep the press informed of your problems, especially if they are humorous or can be used to enhance your firm's image. For example, if your bank's electric doors malfunction and lock open during grand opening festivities one snowy January morning, bundle up your staff and send it back to work. Photograph the tellers smiling above their mufflers as they help customers. Send the picture to newspaper editors with a story about the sensitive controls on the new doors and the burglar-proof glass. Give the local television stations a call, too. If you have several problems with your opening, report them in a humorous "in spite of" feature that points out how well your staff handled the calamities.

Distribute your press releases to every newspaper whose readers might be interested. Send the first press release on the new branch bank to the papers in each city where the bank has branches; to the financial and business papers in the headquarters's city; and to the papers in the city where the branch will open. Send the story about the architects and contractors to their hometowns as well as to the city where the branch is planned. Send the releases on the branch's employees to papers in the towns where these people grew up and where they now live. The releases should also be sent to papers in towns where the employees have recently worked in other bank branches. For example, if your new Walla Walla branch will be managed by a woman who has spent a year as assistant manager at the Renton branch and two years as lending officer at the Federal Way branch, send the story to the Federal Way paper as well as to the Renton and Walla Walla papers.

Organize your publicity program so well that you can adjust it easily when reporters take an interest in your project. If you have a press release on the assistant manager and tellers scheduled for the fourth week preceding the branch opening, revise your schedule if the local newspaper wants to feature these employees as soon as they're selected. Write your release early and send it to every editor at the same time. If you refuse to give a reporter information only because you want to use the material in the next week's press release, you'll be accused of "orchestrating" the news and you'll seriously damage your credibility with the press.

THE OPEN HOUSE AND THE PRESS CONFERENCE

Besides a series of press releases and publicity photographs, some publicity programs include publications, press conferences, talk show appearances and press interviews, open houses and tours. For example, to promote a model home being designed and built for a feature in a magazine like *Better Homes and Gardens* or *Family Circle*, you could issue a series of press releases, hold a press conference, and open the house to the public.

What's the first step with a publicity program like this? Hiring a clipping service and making a carefully planned schedule. By hiring the clipping service before you issue even the briefest press release or speak to a reporter, you will ensure that you obtain copies of everything that's printed about your project. On your schedule include the press releases you'll issue, the renderings you'll draw, and the photographs you'll take. Add the publications you'll write and design, the interviews you'll arrange, the press conference, and the open house. Put your schedule in writing, with deadlines for every job. Type up a list for every day or every week and give copies to everyone who's helping you; or add the jobs to your daily calendar under "Things to do."

Leave wide margins for notes to yourself; jot down which tasks require more time so you can revise the schedule when you plan your next publicity program.

Here are some suggestions for your publicity program.

Press Releases

Your first press release can be a brief announcement of the project, the magazine involved, the local sponsors, the general geographic area of the house site, and the tentative starting date for construction. Send this release to business, real estate, or "home" section editors and to news directors at every newspaper and broadcast station in the city where the house will be built, where the magazine is published, and where the local sponsors are in business. Follow this with a short article on the architects, the contractors, the interior designer, the financing institution, and the house site.

Your third release can be a brief description of the house design; mention the projected magazine publication date and how plans for the house will be sold. Send along a black-and-white rendering of the house. In your fourth release, announce the open house; send a photograph of the house and an invitation to the press conference. Issue follow-up stories that say how many people viewed the house, when the house was sold, and what kind of coverage the project received in the national magazine.

Renderings

If the architect does not provide a rendering in black ink on white paper, commission an illustrator to produce the rendering you need, using the most attractive elevation from the house plans. Have the rendering printed on heavy paper and package it carefully for mailing.

Photographs

Few major newspapers publish construction photographs of projects like model homes. When such pictures are printed, the building is usually near completion and easy to recognize.

Before investing time and money in these pictures, ask the city editors of your local papers if they are interested in construction photographs.

Before the open house, take an exterior picture of the house. Because this will be used to publicize the open house, make the picture as attractive as possible; if you can, photograph the house after all construction, painting, and landscaping have been finished and the site has been cleaned up. This is seldom possible, so plan ahead with the contractor to have at least the front of the house painted and the porch completed before photography. Take your pictures two or three weeks in advance of the open house so editors will have their prints ten days before the event.

When you're photographing a building that is still under construction, hide all equipment and construction materials. Compose the picture carefully to avoid unpainted siding, the concrete forms, the missing trim boards, and the workers. Crop out other evidence of construction when you print the picture. To conceal the lack of landscaping, shoot through trees or over tubs of flowers. For more suggestions on propping, see Chapter 7.

Publications

If you publish a folder or brochure on the project, you will have something to give people at the press conference and the open house. You also can send the brochure to people who inquire about the model home. The brochure can be a simple one- or two-fold publication with a rendering of the house, a sketch of the floor plan, and a description of the special features. Add the names of the magazine, the sponsors, the architects, the contractor, and the interior designer and the telephone number of someone who can provide more information.

Before this publication is printed, you'll need an estimate of the number of people who will attend the press conference and open house. You will need at least one folder for every family (not every individual) that tours the house. To produce the folder, hire a graphic designer and a copywriter unless the architect has provided all the art you need and you have written the text yourself. You'll still need help with the folder design, the typesetting, the mechanical, and the printing. A graphic designer or your printer can handle these and suggest papers and ink colors.

Interviews

Editors and talk show hosts appreciate the opportunity to interview people from other cities and those who are working on newsworthy projects. If you're working on a model home, ask the magazine editors, the architect, and the interior designer if they are willing to be interviewed by local reporters and broadcasters. Try to determine how well these people interview and when they'll have time to meet reporters.

Dee Jones, Editor
Belfair Register
Belfair, Idaho

Dear Ms. Jones:

As you may know, we here at Burke & Co. are working with Home Guides on a model home that will be featured in the magazine's October issue. The two-bedroom house has been designed by Central City architect Owen Davis so that even inexperienced carpenters can handle most of the construction themselves.

Inside, designer Mira Towle has used furniture kits and building plans for furnishings that are just as inexpensive and easy for the do-it-yourselfer.

If you would like to talk to either Mr. Davis or Ms. Towle about how this house's do-it-yourself features make it affordable for even young singles or couples, please call me. I'll be glad to arrange an interview or to make sure that you meet these two talented designers at our press preview of the house on April 16.

Sincerely,

FIGURE 6-1   LETTER TO EDITOR, SAMPLE

When you know who is available for interviews, invite local reporters and broadcasters to talk to the people who will be in town for the press conference. These interviews may take place at the press conference itself, or they may be taped at studios and aired immediately before the open house. To approach a reporter you don't know, write a note explaining the project and suggesting an interview. See Figure 6-1 for an example. Follow up the letter with a call.

The Press Conference

Some press conferences are formal meetings of Fortune 500 company presidents or high-level government officials and representatives of national newspapers, networks, and trade publications. The people who run small businesses seldom make announcements that demand such elaborately staged events. However, there are times when you will find that casual gatherings with local and regional reporters and editors are convenient and worthwhile. You can save time and money by demonstrating a new product or introducing new managers or guest speakers to everyone at once. The reporters benefit, too; they all receive the information at the same time, and they all have the same opportunity to gather the additional material that will make each story a little different.

Schedule your press conference, party, or preview so that reporters from both weekly and daily papers can attend. Plan the conference with an idea of when you would like the stories on your project to be published, too. For example, if you've scheduled your open house for Sunday, you would like the stories on the model home to appear late in the week before— soon enough that people make plans to visit the house but not so early that they forget about it. If you invite reporters to meet with you on the previous Monday, the editors at most weeklies will be able to write their story for that week's edition. At most dailies, the reporters will be starting work on their stories for the larger "home" editions that are published later in the week. A project like a model home is then likely to appear in both weeklies and dailies on Thursday.

Jerry Cummings
Editor, Sound Life
<u>Tacoma News Tribune</u>
Tacoma, Washington

Dear Ms. Cummings:

The roof's on, the rug's down, the rhododendrons are planted:
"The House That Women Built" is finished.

This unique model home, designed by women to meet women's needs,
will be open to the public Sunday, May 8. But to give you an
opportunity to tour the house and meet the people who've been
involved in the American Plywood Association-<u>Family Circle</u>
project, we've scheduled a press conference for Monday, May 2,
at noon at the house.

Here to discuss the house, which will be featured in the September
20 issue of <u>Family Circle</u>, will be Elizabeth Gaynor, <u>Family
Circle</u> home furnishing editor; Carolyn Geise, project architect,
The Hastings Group; Terry Martin, J.C. Penney interior designer
for special projects; and representatives of the American Plywood
Association's Information Services Division. For your pleasure,
Jeff Smith's crew from The Chaplain's Pantry will be serving
special hors d'oeuvres.

Enclosed is a map that'll help you locate the house. If you'd
like more information, just call.

Sincerely,

FIGURE 6-2   INVITATION TO PRESS CONFERENCE

For a press conference, you'll need invitations. These can
be printed or computer-personalized letters like Figure 6-2
that describe the project and tell who will be present. List the
date, the time, and the name of someone who can provide additional information before the press conference. Send along a
map and directions for reaching the model home. The map
should be carefully drawn and the directions clearly written,
because the reporter may use them in his or her story as well
as in the trip to the press conference.

For refreshments, call local caterers and gourmet cooking
schools for estimates and menu suggestions. Tell the caterer
how many people you expect, how long the press conference
will last, how far the model home is from the caterer's kitchen, and what facilities will be available. For example, will
the range, oven and refrigerator be operating? If the interior
of the house has been decorated for display and photography,

how much kitchen counter space will be available? Where can serving dishes be placed?

The press kit may be as simple as a pocket portfolio with one black-and-white exterior photograph of the house, one in-

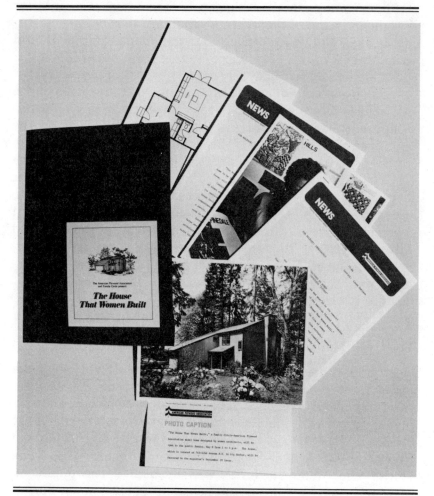

FIGURE 6–3   PRESS KIT

This model home press kit includes press releases, photographs, and floor plans. The material is compiled in a custom folder labeled with an adhesive-backed rendering of the project.

terior shot, a press release on the house design, and an announcement of the open house. It may be as elaborate as a custom-printed presentation folder filled with camera-ready floor plans; photographs and biographical sketches of the editors, architect, contractor, landscape architect, and interior designer; detailed stories on the house and interior design; and a list of those firms supplying the appliances, furniture, floor and wall coverings, custom-made equipment, and special accessories. (For more suggestions on producing a press kit folder, see Chapter 11.)

The press conference should include introductions of the magazine editors and the people involved with the house design and construction. Ask each one to comment on the significance of the project; the builder might mention building systems that cut the construction cost, while the architect could discuss how small rooms were designed to appear larger. Allow time for the reporters to tour the house and to speak to each of the guests. If your group is small or if reporters arrive at different times, ask each person involved with the project to escort a different reporter on a tour. Schedule filmed tours of the house before or after the conference so that broadcasters and their camera crews don't have to work around other reporters.

The Open House

Open houses usually are held on Sundays. If you open the house at noon or in the early afternoon, people can stop on their way home from church or come after brunch or an early dinner. If you can, schedule the open house for a holiday that relates to the house theme. For example, the American Plywood Association–*Family Circle* model home called "The House That Women Built" was opened to the public on Mother's Day. You also might schedule an open house during a local festival or Chamber of Commerce promotion that will attract people to the same area.

Send special invitations to the open house to firms that donated materials and services and to those that lent props and plants for the interiors. For a sample letter, see Figure 6-4.

The roof's on, the rug's down, the rhododendrons are planted:
"The House That Women Built" is finished!

All of you who have helped with this American Plywood Association-
Family Circle model home project have been just great; we'd like
to thank you . . . and we'd like to invite you to a special open
house Saturday, May 7, from 1 to 3 P.M. The house will also be
open to the public Sunday, May 8, from 1 to 4 P.M.

To reach the house, which is located on Pt. Fosdick, follow the
directions on the attached map. If you'd like more information,
please call me.

Sincerely,

FIGURE **6-4**   INVITATION TO OPEN HOUSE

Following a Press Conference

After the press conference and open house, send reporters
and editors pictures of the crowd at the open house, with
a short release on the total number attending. Write casual notes of thanks for their help to those reporters and
broadcasters who featured the project. For a sample, see
Figure 6-5.

Order extra copies of the papers that featured the house.
Compile these stories and those you receive from your clipping service with candid photographs shot at the press conference and the open house. Put the material in a binder for
the magazine editors involved with the project. Send photocopies of the clippings and pictures taken at the open house
to the firms that supplied materials and services for the
house.

When you've obtained the magazine editors' permission
to send stories to trade journals about the house and your
publicity program, put together fact sheets on every
newsworthy angle. Write stories about the house's special
features so that the releases can be mailed to regional con-

Dee Jones, Editor
Belfair Register
Belfair, Idaho

Dear Ms. Jones:

I'm glad you were able to attend the press tour of our model
home last week. All of us from Burke & Co. and Home Guides
enjoyed meeting you. We were also delighted with your story
in last week's paper; I'm sure that's part of the reason we had
so many visitors at Sunday's open house.

As you can see from the enclosed picture, people were lined up
three and four deep most of the afternoon as they waited to
tour the house. By 5 P.M. 1,200 people had visited the project.

Sincerely,

FIGURE **6–5**   FOLLOW-UP NOTE TO EDITOR

sumer magazines and the "home" editors of large daily
newspapers immediately after the magazine story appears.

A PLANT TOUR

Tours of your facilities are another valuable public relations
tool. With a tour, you can show government officials, the
people in your community, and your employees how you
manufacture and distribute products. Use a tour to introduce
yourself in a community where you've opened a new plant
and as a lobbying tactic in a town where you are well
established. You can use a tour to attract new employees, too.

Open your plant to the entire community during a grand
opening or to show off a major addition or improvement. Or
schedule an open house during a local festival or national
observance. For example, a timber company might demonstrate helicopter logging during a local loggers' jamboree; a
veterinarian might offer tours of his or her operating rooms
and kennels during National Pet Week.

Week 1
Engage a clipping service.
Issue the first press release, an announcement of the project.
Request biographical information for a press kit from everyone who will be introduced at the press conference.
Propose tentative dates for the press conference and open house; check the construction schedule, community calendar, and participants' schedules for conflicts.

Week 2
Call the caterers for cost estimates and menu suggestions.
Visit an office supplies store and talk to a printer for information on press kit folders.
Start a list of the firms supplying material and services for the house; check the accuracy of every name listed.
Call rental supply houses for information on stanchions.

Week 3
Issue a press release on the architect, landscape architect, and contractor.

Week 4
Send reminder notes to those who have not provided biographical information for the press kit.
Continue to list suppliers.

Week 5
Commission an artist to produce a rendering and a sketch of the floor plan.

Week 6
Write copy for the brochure on the house; have this text approved by the project sponsors and magazine editors if necessary.
Contract with a caterer.

Week 7
Have the rendering photostatted and printed.
Write a caption for the rendering and have it printed or photo-copied.
Write a press release on the house design to distribute with the rendering and the caption.
Mail the releases, renderings, and captions.
Send the rendering, copy, and a floor plan to a graphic artist for the brochure design and mechanical.
Order a large wood sign for the house site.

Week 8
Review the brochure design and select the ink color and the paper.
Obtain directions to the house and have a map drawn.
Use the telephone calls you've received in response to the press releases and attendance figures at earlier open houses to estimate how many people will visit your model home. Use this figure to determine how many brochures to order.
Ask the architect, contractor, interior designer, and others involved with the project when they will be available for inter-views.

Week 9
Send copies of the brochure mechanical to printers if you want more than one cost estimate. In the specifications, mention paper, ink color, quantity, and the date you need the brochures.
Select a printer and order the brochures.
Invite reporters to interview the people involved with the project.

FIGURE 6-6 TWELVE-WEEK SCHEDULE FOR MODEL HOME
PUBLICITY PROGRAM

FIGURE 6-6 CONT.

Write the biographical sketches for the press kit and submit
them for approval.
Write a press release on the house design for the press kit.
Check on parking for the press conference and open house.

Week 10
Have one exterior photograph taken to send with the press
release on the open house.
Have press conference invitations and maps printed.
Order paper or plastic mats to protect floor coverings in house.
Announce the open house with a press release; send along pictures,
press conference invitations, maps, and information about parking.
Call the reporters you've invited to interview people involved
with the project; schedule meetings before, after, or during
the press conference.
Arrange for someone to sleep in or guard the house while it's
decorated and furnished.

Week 11
Have the printer deliver folders.
Send the caterer a map and directions; call later to confirm
all details.
Call the contractor to ensure that the range, oven, and
refrigerator will be operating.
Have one exterior and one interior photograph taken for the press
kit.
Estimate press conference attendance; use this figure to order
photographs and press kit folders.
Print press releases for the press kit.
Assemble enough press kits for the reporters who attend, for
those who will want the material even though they do not attend,
and for the people involved with the project.
Walk through the house and plan a traffic pattern for the open
house.
Erect the sign at the house.
Buy "no parking" and "no smoking" signs.

Week 12
Before the press conference:
   Load the camera with fast black-and-white film for candid
   photographs.
   Transport the people who are to be interviewed on television
   to the studios.
   Put down paper or plastic mats.
   Put out ashtrays for the reporters and take garbage bags for
   the caterers and general cleanup.
   Have the floor vacuumed and windows washed.
   Station someone at the house to meet caterers.
Before the open house:
   Take a camera with color slide film and black-and-white film
   for candid pictures of people touring the house.
   Put the stanchions in place.
   Post the "no parking" and "no smoking" signs with a staple
   gun; place a large ashtray at the entrance.
   Arrange the folders near the entrance.
   Take beverages, glasses, and toilet tissue for the guides.
   Call the police regarding possible traffic problems during
   the open house.
   Buy a counter to count the visitors.
   Remove valuable or dangerous props.
   Remove faded blossoms in the flower arrangements.

Give tours for your employees and their families, too. In a large plant, where most employees see only their own operations, a tour will improve worker morale; people will see what happens to a product before it reaches them and after it leaves them. With a tour you can emphasize what you're spending on health programs and safety equipment and what absenteeism costs you.

Consider offering regular tours as part of a public relations program. You can schedule daily, weekly, or monthly tours for everyone who is interested. If you prefer, offer tours by appointment only to civic and school groups.

Government officials at all levels visit plants during campaigns. Many also visit local business people during goodwill tours of districts. While walking legislators and other officials through your operations, you can point out which new regulations are hurting your business and your ability to expand; you can emphasize how many jobs you directly and indirectly create in the community and how much you contribute in taxes. Besides giving you the opportunity to lobby, a tour will make you newsworthy; local reporters will be interested in a government official's visit with you. Include an invitation to tour your operation in the letter that you write your legislator about pending bills or current controversies.

Planning the Tour

As you think about a tour, consider what you will show your visitors. Use a floor plan of your plant or a rough sketch of your operations to map out the tour, choosing those areas that illustrate the points you want to make. Keep enough equipment operating to make the tour interesting. Plan to stop in quiet areas to describe the operations. To show maps and charts, you'll need an area where each member of the tour group can see the artwork. For slides, you'll need an area that can be darkened and has chairs.

Now think about how long the tour will be. Remember to allow time for questions. Once you know how long the tour will be, how many employees can serve as guides, and how many people you will want in each tour group, you can determine how many visitors you will be able to accommodate. Multiply the number in each tour group by the number of guides by the number of tours a guide can run each hour. Then multiply this figure by the number of hours of the open house. For example, suppose that you would like to limit each tour group to a dozen people and you have five guides available. If each tour takes thirty minutes and you're planning a three-hour open house, you can handle 360 visitors: twelve in each group multiplied by five guides multiplied by two tours an hour multiplied by three hours. Compare this figure with the number of people you may attract. Estimating attendance is easier if you know how many people have attended similar open houses in the same area. Remember that an open house held during pleasant weather, on a school holiday, or after working hours will probably be better attended than one scheduled for a February weekday afternoon. If you expect attendance at any one time to exceed your capacity, arrange for larger groups, more guides, and a spacious, comfortable waiting area. You may also want to change your last-minute advertising to emphasize the off-peak periods.

If your group is small, you can begin or end the tour with a luncheon at the plant or a nearby restaurant, with pastry and coffee, or with hors d'oeuvres and cocktails. With a larger group like your employees and their families, serve coffee and soft drinks or hot dogs and ice cream bars.

Will you offer your visitors souvenirs or handouts on your company? If so, order these as soon as you've estimated attendance. Use printed material or visual aids to tell your visitors:

how many people you employ;
your average payroll;
what products you make and distribute and which
    markets you serve;
what raw materials you use;
how much you pay in property taxes and in federal,
    state, and local taxes;

how much you spend on environmental problems and
  safety equipment;
how you're conserving energy;
how much you spend locally to buy supplies, materials,
  and services; and
how other industries in your community depend on your
  plant for supplies.

To publicize your open house, you can write press releases and letters to civic, social, and youth groups; you can
arrange for signs on school, business, and community reader-
boards. In your letters and releases, emphasize whether
young children are welcome and if children must be accom-
panied by adults. Mention whether or not you can accommodate the handicapped.

If you run frequent tours, notify the local newspapers
that publish weekly calendars of events and the civic groups
that print tourist brochures. In many large cities, books that
list tours have been published. Look for these guidebooks in
the tourist section of your local bookstore; write the
publishers and ask to have your tour mentioned in the next
editions.

The most valuable stories often appear after the open
house. Make sure that local reporters and broadcasters have
the opportunity to interview officials during or after the tour.
Have your camera available for candid and posed photographs of officials and employees, plant managers, and labor
leaders. Try to catch the "feature" pictures, too; let a long-
retired employee compare the equipment he used with what's
in place now. Photograph a preschool girl as she stares at a
huge press or lathe. Have these pictures processed immediately; send copies to reporters and to everyone pictured.

REMEMBER THE POSTMORTEM

Whether you organize a press conference, an open house, or a
tour, sit down the day afterward and write down:

What's your objective?
    To promote good community relations
    To encourage employee loyalty
    To illustrate company policies and benefits
    To show how your products are made
    To demonstrate free enterprise in action
    To attract prospective employees

Who's in charge?
    You
    Your secretary
    Committees
    Supervisors
    Foremen
    The union
    The public relations department

Who's invited?
    Employees
    Employees and their families
    Customers
    Civic leaders
    Stockholders
    Legislators
    Teachers and administrators
    Suppliers
    Manufacturers
    Dealers
    Retired employees

Setting the date
    A company anniversary
    A local festival
    A national observance
    A school holiday
    Avoid conflicts with other local events

The budget
    How many will attend?
    Refreshments
    Decorations
    Displays
    Name tags
    Souvenirs and prizes
    Overtime pay for preparations, tour, and cleanup

Facilities
    Parking
    Reception area for start of tours
    Flags: United States, State, and company
    Checkroom
    Machinery in good working order

FIGURE 6–7   CHECKLIST FOR A COMPANY TOUR

FIGURE **6-7** CONT.

```
Hazardous areas roped off
Clean vehicles on display
Information signs and arrows
Place for serving refreshments
Public address system
Door prize display and box for stubs
Display of company products and environmental and safety
equipment
Literature racks
Hotel/motel reservations for special guests
Flight schedules and ground transportation for special
guests
```

```
Getting ready
Do a thorough housecleaning
Make a list of speakers and estimate the length of each
speech
Conduct a "dry run" of the tour
Prepare explanations of machines and processes for guides
Prepare a slide show on the company history or products
Order refreshments, paper plates and cups, plastic flatware
Find large wastebaskets for the refreshment area
```

how may people attended;
how many folders and souvenirs you distributed;
how much food was consumed;
the peak periods;
the most popular features of the open house or tour;
the problems you had—and how you can avoid them
    with your next project.

File these notes with copies of your original schedule, clippings, maps, press conferences, and letters of invitation. Jot down the names of the illustrators, graphic designers, printers, caterers, and shops that provided help. Add the names of reporters and editors to your regular office mailing list.

7
PHOTOGRAPHY

Pictures are important: editors, publicists, and your potential clients want to see your projects and products. Good pictures are very important: lenses, lighting, accessories, and background can create photographs that figuratively seduce editors, awards program judges, and customers. With photography you can illustrate what makes your project newsworthy; you can suggest ways to use your product; and you can emphasize its attractiveness. A filter on the lens and a quick spray of water on the lawn will make a building's white siding blindingly bright, the sky a deep blue, and the grass vivid green. A wide angle lens and an unusual camera perspective will emphasize the length of a toy train or the thickness of a bakery's cheesecake. Because editors and publicists receive information on many more projects and products than they can feature, they often select those that have been most attractively photographed.

For people in design and construction, there's another reason to use good architectural photographers. Photographers often work closely with editors, and they'll submit stories to magazines about the projects they've photographed. Because they usually retain the reproduction rights to their work and so are paid every time their pictures appear in print, photographers will submit pictures to many different magazines.

How do you find good photographers? What do they charge? How can you reduce your photography bills? When should projects be photographed? This chapter answers these questions, and it provides suggestions on propping, cropping, models, sets, and release forms. Intended for any business person who needs photography for advertisements, sales literature, publicity stories, slide programs, and presentations to clients, this chapter includes special words of advice for the designer and builder.

FINDING A PHOTOGRAPHER

Finding a good photographer is easy if you have a generous photography budget and unlimited time. Few firms, regardless of their size, have these advantages; surprisingly, time, not money, is the more common problem. Finding a photographer who can shoot a project in the few days between its completion and an editor's deadline is frequently difficult, especially if the photography involves outdoor work.

The first step in finding a good photographer is learning to recognize good photography. Study the pictures in the magazines where you'd like to have your work featured. Most of the pictures will be focused and properly lit, but some will have an extra clarity and drama. To determine who took these, look for the line of very small type above, below, or beside the photograph. This credit line will list, often with a copyright symbol, the photographer or the firm responsible for the picture. Projects built in your area may have been shot by a local photographer; compare the names in credit lines with listings in the Yellow Pages or photographers' directories.

Many products featured in consumer magazines like *Family Circle, Better Homes and Gardens, House Beautiful,* and *Popular Mechanics* are photographed in the magazines' own studios or on location by photographers selected by the editors. To reach such a photographer, call or write the editor whose name appears on the same feature. Ask for the photographer's address and telephone number; if the credit line only lists a firm, ask for the name of the photographer who handled the assignment.

To find an architectural or commercial photographer, ask other business people whom they use. Call advertising agencies, editors, and publicists for recommendations. Don't hesitate to ask other people what they pay, but remember that some photographers reduce their rates for regular customers and the editors of prestigious magazines. Before you commission a photographer, invite the photographer to your office to show you his or her portfolio and to discuss fees, film and processing charges, and rights. If you have a specific photography job in mind, describe it to the photographer. Show him or her a sample of the product or plans of the project. Describe the pictures you would like: close-ups, night shots, exteriors, interiors, step-by-steps. Mention the problems you expect with each shot. Will the photographer have to work with a package mock-up to show a new product? Will he or she have to climb onto a roof to show your building's facade? When you ask for a cost estimate on architectural photography, ask if the photographer would like to visit the site.

If you can't find an experienced photographer in your area, you have two other options: fly someone in or train a promising local photographer. Bringing in a photographer is expensive; you'll pay travel expenses in addition to a day rate that may exceed $1,000. However, many photographers travel frequently; you can obtain their travel schedules by writing or calling them. If a photographer comes to your area with several assignments, you can share the travel expenses with other clients.

Training a photographer to shoot exactly the pictures you need is a time-consuming process. Because you assume so much risk and invest so much time, try to keep the photographer's fees low. Instead of a day rate and the film costs, offer to pay the film costs and a $50 or $75 fee whenever a magazine publishes one of the pictures. (With payments from you and from the magazine, beginners who quickly learn what editors want can make more money than they can if they work on a day rate.) To find a photographer who is interested in your projects, talk to the instructors at local photography schools and other business people who commission photography. Call the photographers who advertise for general commercial work, too.

As you work with photographers, develop a list of the people you like best. Jot down their rates, their idiosyncracies, and the geographic areas they cover. Add clippings of photographers' work and the recommendations you receive from editors. You'll find a file like this particularly valuable if you commission photography in different parts of the country and must hire several photographers.

WHEN YOU COMMISSION A PHOTOGRAPHER

When you commission a photographer, provide as much information about the job as you can. If the photographer will be shooting a product that is to be pictured in an advertisement, provide a mock-up of the ad. Specify what part of the product or package you want to emphasize. If you've hired a photographer to shoot a building, provide a copy of the site and floor plans. Show him or her the snapshots you've already taken of the project and provide a list of the pictures you want. For example, if you're having a hospital photographed, you might ask for a shot of the facade, a close-up of the entry, and views of a nurses' station and the therapy room. For a condominium, you may want a picture of the entire building, a view of one unit's entrance, and interiors of the model's kitchen and living room.

If you're unable to accompany a photographer when he or she shoots a building, arrange for the building manager, leasing agent, or someone involved with the project to help the photographer. If the photographer will be shooting someone's office or apartment instead of a model, make sure that you know which unit you'll be showing and that you have the occupant's permission. Tell the photographer how to reach you during the day if he or she has problems.

When you commission a photographer to take the pictures for an annual report, a benefits brochure, or another corporate publication, provide a dummy of the publication. You may want to ask the graphic artist who designed the publication to serve as art director for the photography. The artist and the photographer can work together to select models and plan pictures.

WHAT AND WHEN TO SHOOT

When you will have a "before" and "after" story to tell, photograph the project before any work starts. This is particularly important with renovation and restoration features. Sometimes you can take these pictures yourself, using both color slide film and black-and-white film.

You will occasionally need "in progress" photographs that illustrate steps in construction and manufacturing, especially if your story will appear in a how-to or technical journal. If these pictures will be a small part of the final feature, shoot them yourself. However, if the most important news element in your story is the process or technique, bring in a professional who will have the lamps, lenses, and other equipment necessary for the sharp, well-lit pictures you want. Schedule this "in progress" photography so that it does not disrupt all construction or production work. For example, if you must take a photographer with tripod and lamps into a factory, try to do your shooting near the end of a shift.

Whatever you're photographing, select and plan your setting carefully. If you're photographing outdoors, this is especially important. The lushness and bright colors of landscaping enhance every picture. Blades of grass and flowering trees often hide minor problems like paint chips or stains, electrical outlets, and power meters. If you're photographing a small project like a piece of furniture, borrow a friend's garden or—with written permission from the appropriate authorities—use a city, state, or national park. In exchange for a credit line, you may be able to borrow the facilities of a local restaurant, amusement park, or museum. Use local farmers' fields, too; photograph your product in the midst of tulips, wheat, or Christmas trees.

To compile a list of possible settings, ask your photographer for suggestions and read the credit lines that identify sites in magazine features, advertisements, and the catalogs issued by specialty stores. Ask the Chamber of Commerce and your local or regional tourist bureau for the names of restaurants, hotels, resorts, museums, and parks where you can photograph projects. If you have friends with classic cars, Japanese gardens, or sailboats, ask for their help. Another source of information: your state government. Most states now have officials who find sites for moviemakers; these people, who often work in departments like "economic development," may be willing to help you, too. When you want to photograph your products in a barn or at a farmer's roadside fruit stand, ask the agricultural loan officer of your bank for the names of farmers who may allow you to use their fields. Or call the county extension office or the local office of the federal Soil Conservation Service for help. (Offer your business as a setting for other firms' photography projects, too; you'll benefit from the credit lines you receive and the people you meet.)

Because photography is intended to make a project or product look attractive, consider the work schedule for whatever you're shooting when you plan the photography session. When you photograph a product, try to wait until you have the finished product and the actual packaging. When you photograph a building, try to wait until all of the construction has been completed and the furniture has been delivered.

Often you can't wait to photograph a project until the landscaping is in and the plants are blooming. Some owners can't afford landscaping immediately; others prefer to wait until spring to seed lawns and plant shrubs. Some projects should be photographed as soon as they're completed, before different colored drapes are hung at windows and parking lots are filled with cars. When a project hasn't been landscaped, substitute tubs of plants. Bank the porch or the balcony of a house or small office building with potted geraniums or chrysanthemums. Buy a few small flowering trees and "plant" them, their root balls still wrapped, wherever they're needed. Move them for every picture. Frame your pictures with branches of existing trees or with sprigs held by your assistant.

Wherever you shoot, watch for overhead lines, commercial and traffic signs, and parked cars. Try to have signs moved; ask the people who work in the building to park their cars in another lot for a few hours. Inside a building, remove or conceal extension cords and electrical outlets; move furniture and carefully position artwork, plants, and models. Encourage your photographer to arrange furniture and accessories for the attractive interior photographs so important to most stories. Add furniture, art, pillows, flowers, plants, and baskets if the rooms are sparsely furnished. Borrow furniture from your office or rent it from local stores for a modest fee (offer ten or fifteen percent of the retail price) and the possibility of a credit line if the project is published. Rent the plants from a local florist; for an extra fee, the florist may deliver and pick up the large plants you use to fill corners. Decorate children's rooms with kites, posters, and stuffed animals rented from a toystore; fill shelves with books borrowed from a used bookstore or bought at Goodwill.

If you photograph several projects a year, start a list of the firms that will lend you furniture, china, flatware, baskets, flowers, plants, garden equipment, art, toys, and books for pictures. Write down the fees you usually pay and the people you contact. You'll also want to note the stores where you buy the fresh flowers, fruit, vegetables, posters, calendars, candy, and other props. On each list, include the stores' hours and telephone numbers; you'll want to know that divinity or daffodils are in stock and that the store is open before you leave your office or the photography studio. (When you borrow or rent props, send the merchants thank you notes; if you can, send them copies of the articles in which their products are shown.)

To add color to pictures of rooms with fireplaces, stuff newspaper behind a log or two in the fireplace; douse the paper with lighter fluid and then, seconds before the shutter clicks, light the paper for a brief, bright blaze. Decorate a table with a bowl of fruit, flowering plants, or place mats, china and flatware. Add contrast to a kitchen photograph by spreading a salad bowl, tomatoes, mushrooms, radishes,

FIGURE 7-1   EXAMPLE OF PROPS

Entry
     Door mat
     Planters with flowering plants or shrubs
     Hanging baskets of flowers
     Drapes inside the windows
     Mailbox
     Wreath or Indian corn for door

Deck/Patio
     Lawn chairs, table, and umbrella
     Pillows
     Barbecue
     Casual china or paper plates, pitcher, glasses, and flatware
     Cloth napkins
     Planters with flowering plants or shrubs

Foyer
     Prints, posters, and photographs (framed without glass, if
     possible)
     Fresh flowers and plants
     Area rug
     Coatrack
     Umbrella stand

Living Room
     Books and bookends
     Fresh flowers and plants
     Couch and chairs
     End tables and lamps
     Coffee table
     Prints, posters, and photographs
     Fabric stretchings, quilts, baskets, and straw fans for the
     walls
     Logs and paper for the fireplace
     Basket of firewood
     Candlesticks and candles

Dining Room
     Place mats and cloth napkins
     China, flatware, and crystal
     Centerpiece: a plant or fresh or dried flowers
     Candlesticks and candles
     Table and chairs

Kitchen
     Salad greens
     Cutting board
     Knife
     Loaf of French bread
     Canisters
     China, flatware, and crystal
     Salad bowl

FIGURE 7-2   LIST OF EXAMPLE PROPS

FIGURE 7-2 CONT.

Salt and pepper shakers
Cruets for oil and vinegar
Baskets, posters, fabric stretchings, and a calendar for the walls
For open shelves: stoneware; colorful cans of olive oil, crackers, cookies, and other foodstuffs; and glass canisters filled with oatmeal, peanuts, spaghetti, navy and pinto beans, puffed rice, raisins, jelly beans, spices, and herbs.

Adult's Bedroom
Bed and dresser
Comforter or bedspread
Pillows and pillowcases
Lamps
Posters, photographs, or fabric stretchings for walls
Flowers, plants, and cologne for the top of the dresser
Clothes, shoes, hats, scarves, and umbrella for the closet

Child's Bedroom
Bed or crib
Quilt and sheet
Books, dolls, teddy bears, and other stuffed toys
Building blocks, coloring book, and crayons
Bulletin board, sampler, or fabric stretching for walls
Clothes, shoes, and diapers for closet
Baby oil, baby powder, and cotton balls for the dressing table

Family Room
Chairs and tables
Pillows
Area rug
Bowl of popcorn
Monopoly or Scrabble game
Basket filled with balls of yarn and knitting needles
Books and bookends
Plants and flowers

Bathroom
Towels and washcloths
Soap and toilet tissue
Shower curtain and rings
Plants
Glass jars filled with decorative soaps, shells, cotton balls, bubble bath beads, and epsom salts for the top of vanity or open shelves.

scallions, red and romaine lettuce, and a head of cauliflower across the counter or cutting board. Cut a few slices off a cucumber and then leave the knife by the vegetables as if you'd just been interrupted. For an example, see Figure 7-1; the bread, cheese, tomatoes, and mushrooms on the table add contrast to the green vegetables and the leafy background. For more suggestions on propping, see Figure 7-2.

FORMATS AND COSTS

Commercial photographers ordinarily use 35mm, $2\frac{1}{4} \times 2\frac{1}{4}$-inch, and 4×5-inch black-and-white negative and color transparency film. Some photographers prefer 2×2-inch "super slides" and $2\frac{1}{4} \times 3\frac{1}{4}$-inch film. Because larger negatives and transparencies require less enlargement for 8×10-inch prints and magazine cover pages, they usually make better quality pictures; some editors still accept only 4×5-inch transparencies for publication. You will want slides for submittals to magazines, for presentations, for printing jobs, and for awards program entries. You will want black-and-white negatives so you can have prints for publicity releases, awards programs entries, and office displays.

If your photographer will (some won't) expose 4×5-inch transparencies, black-and-white negatives, and slides every time he or she sets up a picture, you'll have high quality photographs in every format. You can have slide film made from large transparencies and black-and-white prints made from color negatives and transparencies, but neither the slides nor the prints will have the clarity of originals. You'll save money with original slides and black-and-white negatives, too. Because not all labs are equipped to make slides from large format transparencies, you might pay as much as $5 for a good copy—ten times the cost of the film for an original. A copy negative from a 4×5-inch transparency can be five or ten times the cost of a sheet of 4×5-inch black-and-white film.

If you plan to submit photographs of your project to several magazines and awards programs, ask the photographer to double or triple shoot, making two or three identical exposures of every shot. For the warm pictures with good resolution that many editors prefer, ask the photographer to use Kodachrome film or warming filters with Ektachrome.

Whether you need color prints depends on how you plan to use the photographs. Few editors accept color prints, even 8 × 10-inch prints of professional quality. Color prints are difficult and expensive to reproduce with most printing processes. But you can use prints in awards program submittals, sales presentations, and office displays. Framed or matted, they also make excellent gifts for clients. You can substitute color prints for slides in your first letter to an editor about a project, too. Shoot original color negatives (probably with a 35mm camera) or have prints made from color transparencies. When you order a Type R print, it will be made directly from the transparency; when you ask for a more costly C print, the lab will first make an internegative from the transparency, and then will make the print from that. This will give you a higher quality photograph.

A photographer usually keeps the black-and-white negatives he or she shoots. The photographer will send you proof sheets from which you can select the pictures you want to have printed. The first print made from a negative usually costs more than each of the subsequent prints from the same negative because the photographer charges you for darkroom setup time. To reduce your photography bill, estimate how many copies of the same picture you will need for awards program entries and press releases; order all of them at the same time. For example, suppose you plan to enter a project in five awards programs during the next eighteen months. If you place five separate orders for the six pictures you need for each binder, you may pay $15 for each print, a total of $450. If you order all the prints at once, you may pay $15 for each of the first prints and $10 for each of the subsequent prints. This reduces your bill to $330.

For processing the black-and-white film you shoot yourself, find a good lab or a photography student who will develop and print your film in his or her darkroom. Don't take the film to your neighborhood drugstore; it will be processed in batches with other film in an automated, high volume plant. You will also need a good reproduction lab that can make the duplicate transparencies and 35mm conversions you will occasionally need.

COSTS AND RIGHTS

Good photography can be expensive. Photographic equipment is costly. Film and photographic paper are expensive because they're made with silver and petroleum-based products. Processing film and printing photographs, like the actual picture-taking, requires skill, time, and expensive equipment. When a camera is used on a tripod or with lamps, each shot must be planned, framed, checked (usually with a Polaroid snapshot), and then readjusted. A photographer may take an hour to set up and photograph each view with black-and-white and color film. These costs must be passed on to you. You usually will be billed for:

> the photographer's time, a standard rate that may range from $45 an hour to $2,000 a day;
> travel expenses, including mileage, meals, and lodging;
> travel time;
> proof sheets;
> film and processing costs (often marked up);
> prop purchase or rental arranged by the photographer; and
> state sales tax.

You should receive:

> one set of numbered black-and-white prints or a set of proof sheets;
> the original color transparencies;

This note will serve as a confirmation of our agreement on the photography of the Cityville Bank.

I want the building to be photographed with 4 x 5-inch color transparency and black-and-white negative film and with 35mm color transparency film. Double shoot the 35mm. I need at least three exterior and two interior photographs no later than December 10.

I understand that I'll receive sets of the 4 x 5-inch and 35mm transparencies and proof sheets of the black-and-white pictures. You will retain the black-and-white negatives and the copyright on all pictures.

Your fee will be $750, mileage at thirty-five cents per mile, and normal film and processing costs. I authorize you to spend as much as $50 on incidental props needed for photography.

I understand that these fees include no reprint rights for national magazines but that I can use the pictures in my own brochures and with press releases to newspapers and local and regional magazines.

If you have any questions about these terms, call me before you photograph the bank.

Sincerely,

I have read this letter and accept the terms stated.

_____, photographer.

FIGURE 7-3 LETTER OF AGREEMENT FOR PHOTOGRAPHY

35mm slides; and
use rights for your own presentations, for brochures,
and for publicity in newspapers and the local and
regional magazines.

Photographers ordinarily retain the copyright on the pictures. They expect to be paid second use or reproduction fees if any of the pictures are published in national magazines or in sales literature and advertisements. Discuss rights before you hire a photographer; for an additional fee, you often can purchase all rights and negatives for pictures that you will use frequently. Whatever your agreement with the photographer, confirm it in writing. Use a letter like Figure 7-3.

If photographers do not provide everything that you have ordered, if their equipment malfunctions, or if the pictures are poor by general standards, ask them to reshoot the job at no charge. Before you complain about pictures, however, remember that their quality is affected by many factors the photographer can't control. Weather and light often cause problems that are difficult to work around; so do nearby construction projects, overhead wires, damaged or weathered building materials, cars, landscaping, and inappropriate furnishings. Careful planning before the shooting is required to handle these problems.

CUTTING COSTS

Because photography can be so costly, plan your expenditures carefully, using a form like Figure 7–4. When you know how many projects you want to photograph, think about how you can cut the cost. To reduce setup charges in the darkroom, remember to order several prints of the same picture at one time. Ask the photographer for original 35mm slides and black-and-white negatives instead of ordering conversions from large format transparencies. Ask editors what size transparencies they want and how many pictures they need so that you can order exactly what will be used.

You can also reduce your photography bill by:

taking the pictures yourself;
ordering only black-and-white prints;
negotiating a special rate for several projects;
sharing the photography costs with others who have
worked on the same project;
finding a trade association or manufacturer that will
photograph the project; and
finding a photographer who will photograph the project
on speculation.

Taking the Pictures Yourself

If you can use a camera with an adjustable aperture and shutter speed, you can learn to take well-focused, clear black-and-white photographs and color slides. Your pictures may lack

Project	Photographer & Time Estimate	Cost Estimate	Shooting Date	Comments
St. Paul's Medical Center	Mike Roberts, half-day	$ 500	5/81	Need additional exteriors.
Lowell Library	M. Roberts, full day	$1,000	5/81	Interiors and exteriors.
Welling Manor	Eric Hoffman, full day	$1,000	5/81	Interiors and exteriors. Developer will share costs.
Wayland house	Home Guides staff photographer		ASAP	Call magazine when landscaping is in.

FIGURE 7-4 ESTIMATING SHEET, PHOTOGRAPHY ASSIGNMENTS AND EXPENSES

the drama of a professional's work, but they will illustrate existing conditions and construction steps. Use these pictures to show editors and publicists your work; determine their interest in a project before you invest hundreds of dollars in professional photography.

You don't need expensive equipment, although you shouldn't try to use an instant-loading or self-developing camera. Many amateurs and professionals use 35mm cameras for which wide angle and telephoto lenses can be purchased. If you prefer a larger format, look at the single lens reflex (SLR) Hasselblad or the sturdy twin lens reflex cameras made by companies like Yashica and Rollei. The $2\frac{1}{4}$-inch-wide film these cameras require is easy to work with if you're learning to process your own film. They're also easier to focus for some people who wear eyeglasses; they have larger viewing screens, and some are equipped with magnifying lenses for focusing. The Hasselblad, for which a variety of different lenses can be purchased, is expensive; in 1980 the basic camera sold for about $2,500. Yashicas and Rolleis do not have interchangeable lenses, and because they're no longer popular, they are difficult to find. But they're much less expensive; the best Yashica twin lens reflex purchased new in 1980 cost less than $250. Used models are even cheaper.

With a sturdy tripod, you can use whatever natural light is available for your pictures. If you are a beginner, shoot one roll of film for every one or two pictures you need. Photograph every setup several times; try different angles. Bracket every shot; besides shooting at the shutter speed and aperture indicated by your light meter, shoot after you've opened the aperture one more f-stop and again after you've closed it one more f-stop. For example, if your light meter indicates that an aperture of f-22 and a shutter speed of 1/125th second are correct, shoot at that setting and at f-32 and at f-16. Always use a cable release and, when the camera is not on a tripod, a shutter speed of at least 1/125th second; both will prevent your body movements from blurring the picture.

If you are not using a camera with through-the-lens viewing, you should also correct for parallax when you position the camera. Parallax, which results from the viewing lens being higher than the camera lens, is what causes you to cut the tops off buildings and the heads off people.

To reduce your film costs, buy only the newest film available; check the expiration date stamped on the end of each carton. If you can obtain a quantity discount, buy film by the case; wrap it tightly in plastic bags and store it in the refrigerator or freezer. The cold will retard the film's deterioration.

If you are not processing the pictures you take yourself, ask your lab for proof sheets. Because these are made by laying the actual negatives on sheets of photographic paper, each picture is exactly the same size as the negative. Use a magnifying glass or a loop magnifier to check the focus of a picture and the details it shows. With a grease pencil or china marker, indicate the shots you would like enlarged and how you would like them cropped.

Only Black-and-White Prints

Ordering only black-and-white photography will save you money. Black-and-white film requires less light than color and so can often be used without lamps; this reduces camera

```
Film
      Are you using the correct film?
      Is the camera loaded?
      Is the film advancing correctly?
      Is the light meter set for the type of film that you're
      using?
Camera
      Is the lens cap off?
      Are you holding the camera straight or is it mounted straight
      on the tripod?
      Have you corrected for parallax?
      Have you connected your cable release, and when the camera
      is not on a tripod, are you using a shutter speed of at
      least 1/125th second?
Focus
      Are you avoiding glare from the sun?
      Have you focused carefully on your subject, using lettering
      or a pattern as a guide?
```

FIGURE 7-5 CHECKLIST FOR BEGINNING PHOTOGRAPHER

setup time. Most photographers also include the cost of black-and-white processing in their fees; if color film is sent to a lab, the cost of processing it is added to your bill.

Most newspapers and some awards programs require only black-and-white pictures. Some publications use little or no color photography because it requires a more expensive, time-consuming production process than black-and-white. Black-and-white pictures can be very dramatic; the starkness can reveal details and emphasize design. However, most magazine editors prefer color. Many consumer magazines use little else, and most trade and professional magazines are increasing their use of color photography. Slides are optional for some awards program entries and are required for others.

Special Rates

Photographers sometimes will reduce their rates if you give them several assignments at once or if you agree to wait until a slack period in their business. When a photographer has only a few assignments for a trip that he or she has planned, he or she may offer you lower rates to ensure a full shooting schedule.

Sharing Costs

If you are working with another firm that needs pictures for its advertising or publicity programs, try to split the photography costs. If you've built a small office building, share the photography bill with the architect and the landscape architect. If you've designed the interiors for a renovated hotel, split the bill with the hotel owners; they can use the pictures in ads and sales brochures.

When you're part of a group that commissions a photographer, each of you will have features of the building or project that you want to see emphasized in the photography. Although this results in more photographs being taken, each of you still pays less than if you had commissioned the photography on your own. Your client may be happier, too; his or her operations will be disrupted only once for photography.

Whenever pictures commissioned by a group are submitted for publication, credit everyone in the group on the fact sheet that accompanies the pictures. List the project features that are important to each member of the group, too.

Working with Associations and Manufacturers

As Chapter 4 points out, many trade associations and manufacturers feature photographs of projects in advertisements, sales literature, and publications. The publicists who work for these associations and manufacturers need good photographs, both for these features and for the publicity stories that they send newspapers and magazines about their products. To get these pictures, publicists often commission photography. If your project is photographed by an association or manufacturer, you can usually borrow pictures from the publicity department or order prints for your own use from the photographer. If a publicist only wants one or two pictures of your project, you probably can split the photography bill with her.

Photographers Who Work on Spec

Some photographers who know product publicists and editors well work "on spec" or as "scouts." They photograph projects at no charge to you because they expect to sell the pictures to an association, manufacturer, advertising agency, or magazine. Because they work so closely with publicists and editors, some photographers who do speculative work are called by manufacturers and magazines that need specific pictures. Even if you don't have projects that are ready for photography, get to know the people who shoot on spec. They're a valuable source of advice, because they understand what kind of pictures are needed for magazine features and advertisements. If you keep a spec photographer informed about your work, he or she may discuss it with editors or even photograph it.

Remember that a photographer who shoots a job on spec has several hundred dollars of time and film invested; the photographer owns the pictures and probably will sell them to whoever pays the most and the soonest. (Some magazines pay photographers when they accept their pictures; others wait until the pictures are actually published.) When a photographer sells the pictures of your project, he or she probably won't worry about finding a magazine that will give you the best exposure. However, because they are paid every time a picture is published, photographers will try to market pictures to several magazines. You may receive publicity in many different publications for several years without investing anything; you probably won't even pay for the postage to submit pictures to editors.

MODELS AND RELEASE FORMS

Should you use models in your pictures? If you want to illustrate how to use a product or if you want to show its size, yes. If you're entering an awards program or want pictures that can be used for many years, no. When you're commissioning photography for a magazine feature, ask the editor what he or she prefers.

The best models are easygoing people who don't mind photographers' egos, the time-consuming and often uncomfortable setups, the contrived settings, and the bright, hot lights. They relax in front of the camera, and they cooperate with your demands for infinitesimal changes in pose. You can use professionals, but employees and friends (and their children) often make excellent models too. When you're shooting how-to pictures, use someone who thoroughly understands what you're demonstrating. For example, when you photograph a cabinet during construction, use the cabinetmaker as a model.

When you select models for a picture, look for people who are similar in height, weight, and frame size. If you're planning a picture with children, look for models who are about the same size and age; they will be easier to pose because they will look alike and will all have mastered the skills that you need. (For example, if the children that you've selected have all reached a certain stage of development, each one will be able to use the toy you're demonstrating.)

When you decide to use people you know as models, plan your picture in detail and decide whom you want to see in the picture before you ask anyone to model. Be prepared to defend your choice with specific professional reasons when other friends or employees ask why you haven't invited them (or their children) to model. When you need children for your pictures, look for well-behaved, confident youngsters who will cooperate with your requests and relax in front of the bright lights and strange equipment. Most children are attractive when they're clean, rested, and dressed well; for the best pictures, however, find a child with good coloring, thick hair, and large eyes. Children between two-and-a-half and three years old usually make good models after they become accustomed to the set. When you select children for pictures, think about their parents. The best parents deliver the child to the studio or location freshly bathed and on time. They help dress the child for photography and then disappear to another room or building so they don't distract or try to discipline the child during the photography session.

When you work with children, be adaptable. Give the children toys or crackers and let them explore the set at their own pace. Unobtrusively follow them with a camera; you'll probably get several candid pictures that you'll like as well as the posed shots that can be taken later.

When you use models, try to work where they will be comfortable. If you're in the studio, provide chairs and coffee for breaks during the shooting; make sure that the models have a place to change their clothes and a well-lighted, clean bathroom. Keep juice and animal crackers on hand for children. (In the summer, keep Popsicles and ice cream in the freezer.) Remember a soft towel for washing youngsters' faces after lunch. When you're working outdoors, you'll need a nearby changing room and bathroom, thermos bottles of coffee and hot chocolate, and somewhere to run—a car, a restaurant, or a picnic shelter—when a cold wind blows or threatening clouds turn into a rainstorm. If you're working with children, try to start work early while the children are still fresh; stop for cookies, cocoa, or lunch when they are tired or cranky. Encourage parents to take a long walk or to return to their cars with a fast-paced novel or the daily paper.

If you include people in pictures that are to be published, whether in magazines, advertisements, or your own brochures, have the models—professionals, friends, or employees—sign release forms. When children are photographed, have their parents sign the forms. Use a release like Figure 7-6, the form used by architectural and commercial photographer Bob Strode. Send a copy of the signed release to any editor who plans to use the photographs. File the original release with the pictures or with your other legal documents. No release forms are necessary when a model can't be identified; you don't need a release for how-to pictures that show hands completing a project.

PRODUCT PHOTOGRAPHY

Small products and projects are often photographed in studios. Extra-wide heavy paper or fabric may be unrolled from the ceiling to create a backdrop without the "seam" of a wall meeting the floor. When the picture has been taken, the background is rolled up again. Many studios also have walls where the wall-floor seam has been hidden by the construction of a special curve of concrete or plaster. When products are photographed with a seamless background, they appear to float. They can be spotlit with a drama not possible with most sets. These clutter-free photographs are especially effective in advertisements where type is superimposed on the pictures. A photographer can also produce clean, shadowless pictures by shooting products on a sheet of glass. When the glass is suspended over a white card, the subject appears to be outlined; no drop-out mask is needed. (A drop-out mask is an acetate cutout used to eliminate shadows, reflections, or

Date _____

For the value received $_____ , I hereby give Strode
Photographers the right to use photographs of _____
either in whole or in part or original or modified form as often
as desired for any and all advertising, trade, or art purposes.
I have right of approval and can release Strode Photographers
or its clients from all claims which I may or can have because
of use or publications.

Signature _____

Address _____

FIGURE 7-6   MODEL RELEASE

background.) Another suggestion: mount your product on
long nails or sticks on the studio wall. With the correct
lighting and camera angle, you'll obtain a picture with no
shadows, even from the supports.

You can also photograph your products as part of a
single wall setting. This more realistic setting, a bit like a
stage set, is especially appropriate for photographs of small
pieces of furniture and wall coverings. You may only need a
wall or a coordinated floor covering and baseboard with furniture and accessories. Other sets usually include two walls
and the floor, and sometimes a third wall and a ceiling for
some pictures. Although these sets are expensive to build
and decorate and they often require large studios, they provide realistic pictures without the problems of photographing
in an existing building. With a set you don't have any electrical outlets or furnace registers; you don't have curious
passersby or traffic noise; and you can control the placement
of every window—and the view from the window.

To design a set, start with a rough sketch of the room
that you want to create and the product that you're il-
lustrating. Doodle in the furniture, drapes, flowers, and accessories. Note the dimensions of the furniture you already
have and the dimensions you prefer for the pieces that you'll
borrow or rent. If one of your props is a four-foot-long
bookcase with twelve inches between shelves, you'll need

books that are eight to eleven inches tall at the spine. To estimate the number of books you'll need, multiply the number of shelves by the four-foot length; then, when you pick out the books, mentally measure the stacks in feet. When you build the set, remember it isn't a room you'll live in—it's an illusion for the camera. Because of the lenses your photographer uses, you may have to hang one window higher

FIGURE 7-7 PHOTOGRAPHY SET IN STUDIO
Note one pair of curtains has been used to suggest two different windows; curtains are hung at different heights to compensate for the camera angle.

than another to make them look the same height in the picture; you may have to spread the flatware in a table setting inches away from the china. To determine how to place your props, put the camera on a tripod and look through it frequently. Or work with someone who will tell you where to place windows and how far apart to move the knives and forks. Remember that sets are not constructed as well as real buildings, either; floors may not be level or corners square. Correct for these problems if you're using a striped wall covering, wainscoting, mobiles, or wall-hung lamps. Make sure that walls are braced to support paintings or wall-hung furniture.

FIGURE 7-8 THE FINISHED PHOTO

When you make out your shopping list for props, always put down more than you expect to use. Because camera lenses "stretch" rooms, it is hard to overprop. Use colors that you might not use in a real room; wallpaper a bathroom in black and white and try fire engine red towels and toiletries. Photograph a white table against a midnight blue wall, a natural wood desk against a kelly green wall, or a tomato-bright bench out on the lawn. For some ideas, check a color wheel; combine colors that are opposite each other, like yellow and purple, blue and orange, red and green. If you use different sets of complementary colors, you'll have enough contrast for black-and-white pictures; combine a pumpkin-colored cake with a navy platter or a glass of burgundy wine with a spring green tablecloth. Or try a monochromatic color scheme, where most of your props are different shades of the same color; for example, with pale lemon walls and an ash straight chair, you might show bright yellow chrysanthe-mums and cushions covered in yellow and gold calico. The smaller the set, the fewer the colors; on a small set limit yourself to two or three colors along with neutrals like natural wood, black, white, and gray. Before you order paint, review your color choices with the photographer; a good photographer will know if dark blue will turn black and if he or she can reproduce the green you want to use. Choose con-trasting colors for the models and their clothes as well as for the background and the props. For some examples of sets that were designed for good reproduction in black and white or in color, see Figures 7–9 and 7–10. In Figure 7–9, a preschooler dressed in a yellow-and-red-trimmed green dress posed with a toybox in a corner set. The toybox is bright blue with white letters; the tray is green. The pale blue walls and white carpet add contrast, but introduce no new colors to the set. The red, yellow, and orange blocks repeat the colors of the dress. Figure 7–10 shows a white table photographed against a seamless orange background. The orange poppies on the napkins and the tomatoes in the salad pick up the color of the wall; for contrast, there's green in the lettuce and in the napkin border; brown in the salad bowl, servers, and plates; and the gray of the stainless steel flatware.

FIGURE **7-9** EXAMPLE OF PROPS 1

On Location

Occasionally you'll want to photograph a product or a project in or near an existing building. Locations add the color and excitement of reality to your pictures, and they save you the work of designing and building sets. For example, it's much

FIGURE 7-10 EXAMPLE OF PROPS 2

easier to photograph a new wine or a wine cooler in a restaurant's wine cellar than to build racks in a studio and haul in bottles. And it's much more realistic to photograph a fashion model on the yacht club pier than in front of a painted backdrop. Before you decide to use a building or a park for your location, talk to the building owner or manager and study the site carefully. Think about:

how much freedom you'll have to rearrange furniture;
how much equipment you'll be allowed to bring in;
how you'll transport your product and props to the site;
how far the cameras, lamps, battery packs, and products
  must be carried;

how level and dry the ground is;
what light is available;
the potential weather problems;
noise; and
how you'll handle curious bystanders.

CROPPING

The composition of a picture begins with the photographer; he or she selects the angle, background, lenses, and lighting that emphasize certain features of the subject. The composition is completed in the darkroom, where the photographer uses tools like bleaches and high or low contrast papers along with techniques like burning in and cropping. Cropping or cutting away parts of a photograph is a means of eliminating extraneous or undesirable elements like traffic signs and utility wires. It's also a way to highlight one detail: the entry of a building, the collar on a dress, the blossom on a plant, the label on a jar. Cropping makes pictures fit into predetermined formats like the narrow vertical for a two-column-wide newspaper photo and the square mug shot for a "who's news" column.

ON THE JOB WITH A PROFESSIONAL

When you accompany a photographer on a shooting project trip, remember that you're working with a trained professional who has both an ego and idiosyncracies. Some photographers are cheerful, unconcerned people who calmly pack gear into a moving van when a hailstorm interrupts shooting or clean up after child models vomit all over the set. Others are nervous and excitable; they criticize projects, they yell and swear, and they walk off jobs without notice. Don't add to the photographers' frustration and worry; after you've told them what you need, let them shoot the pictures. Watch for changes in the weather and passersby who may interrupt

Besides camera equipment, extra film, extension cords,
lamps, scrims, and battery packs, take along:
    window cleaner and paper towels
    hammer and tacks
    long straight pins
    a Swiss army knife
    a stepladder
    a level
    large sheets of cardboard for reflecting light and for
    walking on the set
    a vacuum cleaner and shag carpet rake for indoor locations
    heavy shoes, poncho or umbrella, and insect repellent for
    outdoor locations
    folding stools
    a thermos of coffee, lemonade, or cocoa
    candy bars and napkins, and
    toilet tissue

FIGURE 7-11   CHECKLIST FOR SHOOTING ON LOCATION

the photographer. If it's cold, shiver in silence or go sit in the
car; if it's hot, find a wide-brimmed hat and a water fountain.
Wear heavy shoes and a slicker when the morning's damp;
bring along a folding stool or a blanket so that you can sit
down. Don't complain, don't get in the photographer's way,
and don't lock your keys in your car.

8

PHOTO FILING SYSTEMS

Whether you've photographed two projects or two hundred, whether you take your own pictures or hire a photographer, protect your investment by cataloging and filing your pictures. With a filing system, you can quickly find the pictures you want; you can record when pictures leave your office; and you can protect fragile prints and transparencies from damage.

This chapter is intended for every business person who uses photography—for publicity pictures, product catalogs, or advertisements. Here you will find suggestions for labeling and filing prints, transparencies, and slides. You will also find methods of filing project information and recording when pictures have been sent to editors, publicists, advertising agencies, and printers.

FILING PHOTOGRAPHS

Store your photographs in a roomy file drawer so that they won't be wrinkled, bent, or torn. If you use a drawer with a lock, you can control who removes pictures from the file. (For the people on your staff who frequently use pictures to review details, compile a binder of photographs and reprints on each project.) A locked drawer provides some protection against theft and vandalism; however, if you're afraid of burglary or fire, keep your most valuable original transparencies in a safe deposit box. Always store negatives, transparencies, and film in a cool place; because film is made with gelatin, it can be damaged by high temperatures.

For a simple, inexpensive filing system that can be expanded easily, use standard letter or legal size filing cabinets, hanging files, and manila file jackets. Made in letter and legal sizes by companies like Wilson Jones, these jackets are sold in office supply stores. They're made like file folders, but the sides are closed with gussets. Because of the gussets, the file jackets can expand to hold an inch-thick stack of prints without allowing small prints or transparencies to fall out. The tab across the top of the jacket has enough space for a detailed description of the contents.

Protect your prints by storing them between sheets of cardboard that are rubber banded together. If you use paper clips, you may wrinkle the prints; if you tape the cardboard sheets together, you'll have to cut the package apart every time you want a print. File each set of prints made from the same negative separately; mark the shot number or description of the print on the cardboard so that you won't have to open every package of prints to find the ones you want. Slip 4 × 5-inch transparencies into the heavy paper envelopes sold in camera shops. Transparencies of all sizes can also be filed between cardboard or in the transparent plastic photo pages made by companies like Angler's and Prinz. The pages are usually $8\frac{1}{2}$ × 11 inches; they're made with pockets in many sizes ranging from 35mm and $2\frac{1}{4}$ inches to 5 × 7 inches and $8\frac{1}{2}$ × 11 inches. If you have only a few small transparencies like slides of each project, cut the photo pages into thirds or halves. File each portion of a page with the appropriate prints and transparencies. If you prefer to file all your slides together, keep the photo pages in three-ring binders. Use a separate binder for each project or for each kind of product. Or file the slides by job number. Write the shot numbers on the slide mounts and on small adhesive labels; if you attach a label to each pocket of the photo page, you can tell where pictures belong and which slides are missing.

If you have only a few pictures of a project or product, file all of them in one jacket. When you have several prints and transparencies, sort them into separate files by photograph type or topic. Put all the black-and-white prints in one file jacket and all the transparencies in another. Or store "before" pictures in one file and "after" shots in another. Suppose you're filing pictures of a resort development; put the photographs of the pool, tennis courts, golf course, and bridle path in one file jacket, the exteriors of the restaurant and clubhouse in a second, and the interiors of the model condominium units in a third.

To label your files, use each project's name and job number. For example, the files on your resort development might be labeled "8118 Half Moon Bay: Exterior B/W," "8118 Half Moon Bay: Exterior Color," and "8118 Half Moon Bay: Model Interiors, B/W & Color." Label black-and-white negatives, prints, and color transparencies with the project name and shot numbers; use the same shot numbers for identical pictures in black and white and color. If you can, use the photographer's numbers; then the only additional information that you will need to order prints is the photographer's job number. For example, a slide might be marked "8118 Half Moon Bay: C-1." The same shot in black and white would be labeled "8118 Half Moon Bay: B/W-1." This system will be compatible with the job numbers and the project names on your photograph files. You'll also eliminate confusion when two projects have similar names. If you don't use a job number system in your office, file the pictures alphabetically by project name.

Into each file, slip an information sheet on the project. Use a form like Figure 8-1, a copy of the fact sheet that you send editors (see Figure 3-5 for an example), or a 5 × 7-inch index card on which you've written the project name and location, the date of photography, and the photographer's name, address, and telephone number.

LABELING TRANSPARENCIES

When you receive transparencies, they should be mounted as slides or covered with plastic sleeves that protect them from dust, moisture, and scratches. Because transparencies are the original film that went through the camera, they may be labeled only with film numbers. Slides mounted in a lab will have film numbers on the slide mounts.

To label slides with the project name or number, write on the mount. Avoid adhesive labels; they may cause slides to jam in projectors. To mark each slide mount legibly, use a one- or two-inch-wide rubber stamp with the name of the project. Use another stamp to mark each slide with your firm's name. You also can use these stamps to mark the backs of prints.

To mark transparencies that are not mounted, type or stamp the project and photograph numbers on small adhesive labels that can be attached to the sleeves. When you send transparencies to an editor or printer, make sure they're marked with your address as well as your name and the project identification.

Date _____

Check film sizes available:

	4 x 5	2¼	35mm
B & W	_____	_____	_____
Color negative	_____	_____	_____
Slides	_____	_____	_____

From: _____ Department: _____

Project name: _____ Contact: _____

Project address: _____

Project type: _____

Material: _____ Material: _____

Application: _____ Application: _____

Manufacturer: _____ Manufacturer: _____

Material: _____ Material: _____

Application: _____ Application: _____

Manufacturer: _____ Manufacturer: _____

Date photographed: _____

Name and address of commercial photographer: _____

_____

_____ Phone: _____

Name and address of architect: _____

_____ Phone: _____

Name and address of contractor: _____

_____ Phone: _____

Individual, organization, or publication to whom photo(s) are
sent and date sent: _____

Publication use and page(s): _____

_____

FIGURE 8-1 PHOTO FILE INFORMATION SHEET

134

CATALOGING PRINTS

When you order black-and-white or color negative photography, you receive a set of 8 × 10-inch prints or the proof sheets that show every photograph that was taken. The photographer usually labels the back of each print with the job number and the photo number. He or she labels the proof sheet with the job number; each shot is marked with its own number, usually the negative number. You'll need both the job and shot numbers when you order prints from the photographer. With an original proof sheet, you'll have a clear record of these numbers and the pictures that they represent. If you don't receive a proof sheet from the photographer, substitute photocopies of the prints you receive. Use a colored felt tip pen to copy the job and shot numbers on the front of the photocopies.

Clearly label each photograph with the name of the project, your firm, and the photographer. Include the address to which the photo should be returned; some magazines will send back prints as well as transparencies. You can pencil this information on the back of a print; however, because the pressure on a pencil can damage the photo, it's better to use a rubber stamp or adhesive labels. If you stamp directly on the back of a print, avoid the back side of light areas; the dark ink may show through the photographic image. You also can stamp an adhesive label that you apply to the back of the print after adding specific project information. Other suggestions: type individual labels for each photograph or have

---

```
JONES, JONES, & BROWN, INC.
100 Boylston St., Boston MA 02167

Project: _____ #_____

Location:_____

Photographer:_____ #_____
```

FIGURE 8-2   LABEL FOR PRINTS

labels like Figure 8-2 professionally printed or duplicated on a photocopy machine.

A couple of reminders: Don't apply labels with rubber cement. The chemicals in the cement can ruin photographic paper. And don't tape labels and captions to pictures, especially those printed on single-weight paper; if the caption is pulled off carelessly, the tape may damage the photographic paper's backing.

NEGATIVES

When you photograph a project yourself and have the pictures developed and printed or proof-sheeted at a lab, you will receive the negatives. Protect these in the glassine or plastic sleeves available at camera shops. If you have photographed several projects on one roll of film, cut the negatives apart so you'll be able to file them by project. If you leave at least three negatives in each strip, they'll easily feed into an enlarger for printing. Label the sleeve of each strip with an adhesive label on which you've typed the project name and number and the shot numbers. The five 35mm negatives of a project might be marked "8118 Half Moon Bay: B/W 1-5."

WHEN PHOTOGRAPHS ARE REMOVED
FROM THE FILE

To record when and where photographs are sent, use one of several simple methods. When you send pictures to an editor with a cover letter that lists the project names and picture numbers, put a copy of the cover letter in the appropriate photo file. If you're sending pictures of several projects, drop carbons of the letter in each file. Or keep a stack of 3 × 5-inch index cards near your photo file; write down the shot number of any picture removed from the file, the date, and the name of the person to whom the picture was sent. Leave this card in the file jacket until the picture is returned. With these

Project	Photo Numbers	Photo Type	Sent to	Date Out	Date In	Comments
Half Moon Bay	3, 4, 5, 7	4 x 5	Acme Printer	9/15	10/3	
Pine Meadows	3, 5, 7	B/W	Harry Smith	9/1	11/15	
City Library	1, 2, 5	B/W	Graphic Design,	8/28		
	9	35mm	Inc.			

FIGURE 8-3 PHOTO LOG

Note to staff: If you take the last copy of any print from a file, list the photo below so that we can reorder.

Date	Your Name	Project Name and Number	Photo Number	Photographer

FIGURE 8-4 RECORD OF PRINTS NEEDED

methods, you'll have to check each file monthly, quarterly, or annually to determine which pictures have not been returned. A log like Figure 8-3 lets you quickly see which pictures are out; you can keep the pages in a three-ring binder in the front of the photo filing cabinet.

If you're not the only one in your office who has access to the photography files, post a sign like Figure 8-4 on a clipboard hung near the filing cabinet. The people you work with can use it to record the numbers and descriptions of prints that you need to order.

9

AWARDS PROGRAMS AND CONTESTS

Awards are given in nearly every profession and industry. There are Effies and Emmys, Maggies and Cleos, Gold Nuggets and Silver Anvils. There are awards for young professionals and awards for veteran practitioners; there are awards for innovation and awards for preservation. You can receive an award if you're an art director, a beautician, a builder, a film maker, or a fashion designer. You can be honored for a book, a business card, a condominium, a commercial, a newspaper, or a Neuchâtel.

Newspapers and magazines are full of contests, too, and they don't all require proof-of-purchase seals and descriptions of your dream vacation in twenty-five words or less. If you win a magazine's "Prize Pet" contest with a photo of your pooch, or its garden contest with your plans for an easy-care quarter acre, you'll meet magazine editors and you may be able to use the publicity in your business.

Why enter awards programs and contests? The answer is in this chapter. You will also find suggestions on the kind of awards programs and contests to enter, how to use your awards and prizes in marketing, and how to budget for awards programs. You will find out how to cut the cost of entries and whether or not to enter the same project in more than one program at the same time.

WHAT AWARDS PROGRAMS SHOULD YOU ENTER?

Enter the awards programs that are sponsored by representatives of your customers—by the magazines they read and the trade and professional associations to which they belong. When you receive an award, you will have an implicit endorsement from some of the people your customers trust most. If you're an architect who specializes in housing, enter the programs sponsored by *Builder, Housing*, and *Professional Builder*. If you design schools and libraries, enter the programs sponsored by school journals and library associations. If you manufacture building products, get the projects constructed with your materials entered in the programs run by design associations and magazines. Suppose you run an advertising agency; enter your point-of-purchase materials in the marketing program run by a retailing magazine. If you're a free-lance writer, submit your stories to the awards programs run by the trade associations and charities that hire free-lancers.

How do you find the names of these programs? Read the trade journals that serve specific industries; you'll find news stories announcing the winners of one program and the entry deadline for the next one. In many magazines, you'll see advertisements for awards programs; if you subscribe to these magazines, you may also receive entry information by mail. Read your local newspapers carefully, too; they'll list the local people who have received awards in regional and national programs. When you're in your competitors' offices, look at the certificates on their walls and the awards listed in

Award	Eligible Contestants or Entries	Contact
Media		
Golden Hammer	Wire service or free-lance writers, editors, and reporters who write magazine or newspaper articles on housing issues	Director, Media Relations National Association of Home Builders 15th and M Streets, N.W. Washington, D.C. 20005
Editor and Publisher Promotion Awards Competition	Newspaper publishers who develop sales promotion programs	Editor and Publisher 575 Lexington Avenue New York, New York 10022
Public Relations/ Advertising		
Silver Anvil	PRSA members and others in public relations who organize public relations programs	Public Relations Society of America 845 3rd Avenue New York, New York 10022
Financial World Gold Medal	Firms that publish annual reports and public issues advertising	Financial World 919 3rd Avenue New York, New York 10022
Retailing		
Drummer Awards	Manufacturers who develop merchandising programs for building supply retail outlets	Building Supply News Awards Center 5 South Wabash Avenue Chicago, Illinois 60603
Retailer of the Year	Building supply retailers who run unusually profitable and progressive operations	Building Supply News Awards Center 5 South Wabash Avenue Chicago, Illinois 60603
Design/Construction		
Redwood Plywood Imagination Award	Designers of redwood plywood projects	Dean Matthews Advertising and Promotion Manager Simpson Timber Company 900 4th Avenue Seattle, Washington 98164
HUD National Awards for Urban Environmental Design	Public agencies, designers, builders, and developers who have designed or administered HUD-assisted urban projects	Department of Housing and Urban Development Washington, D.C. 20410

142

Golden Nuggets Award Competition	Architects and builders who have designed and built residential, commercial, and industrial projects in fourteen western states	Executive Director Pacific Coast Builders Conference Suite 1407 235 Montgomery Street San Francisco, California 94104
Competition for Young Professionals	Architects, contractors, and engineers thirty-nine and younger who do nonresidential work	Building Design & Construction 5 South Wabash Avenue Chicago, Illinois 60603
CRSI Design Awards	Architects and engineers who design site-cast reinforced concrete structures	Director of Marketing Concrete Steel Reinforcing Institute 180 North LaSalle Street Room 2110 Chicago, Illinois 60601
Progressive Architecture Design Awards	Architects and planners whose projects are in the design development stage	Progressive Architecture 600 Summer Street Stamford, Connecticut 06904
Record Houses	Architects who design houses and apartments	Editor Architectural Record 1221 Avenue of the Americas New York, New York 10020
Plywood Design Awards	Designers and builders who develop projects with structural and aesthetic applications of softwood plywood	American Plywood Association P.O. Box 11700 Tacoma, Washington 98411
Western Home Award	Designers of residential projects in thirteen western states	Awards Editor Sunset Willow & Middlefield Roads Menlo Park, California 94025
AIA-administered programs	Registered architects	Maria Murray American Institute of Architects 1735 New York Avenue, N.W. Washington, D.C. 20006 (There are several programs; write for information)
Landscaping National Landscape Awards Program	Businesses, institutions, and government agencies that contribute to landscape beautification	American Association of Nurserymen, Inc. 230 Southern Building Washington, D.C., 20005

FIGURE 9-1 EXAMPLES OF AWARDS PROGRAMS

their presentation materials. Ask magazine editors and professional associations to add your name to their mailing lists if they sponsor awards programs.

Enter the awards programs run by your professional journals and associations, too. When you receive an award, your competitors and co-workers will be impressed; you'll develop a reputation for award-winning projects. You'll also attract the attention of students looking for jobs and other professionals who need joint venture partners. To find the names of these programs, read your professional journals and newsletters and the bulletins from your associations. In some industries special catalogs of awards are published; for example, the *Building and Design Industry's Awards Directory* lists awards programs for designers and builders.

SIMULTANEOUS AND REPEAT ENTRIES

Because juries differ from program to program and, within the same program, from year to year, projects may receive no recognition in one program and be honored in several others. That's one reason to enter each project in every program for which you and the project are eligible.

Money is another reason to enter the same project in several programs. For example, you'll need a set of black-and-white prints (and possibly a set of slides) for each design awards program you enter, but you'll only pay one bill for project photography. If you order all the prints you need at one time and use the prints from one year's entry binders when you enter the next year's programs, you'll save even more. Suppose you submit the pictures of your new office building to five awards programs as soon as the building is completed. If the photographer charges you $750 to shoot the building, $15 for each of the first prints made from six negatives, and $10 for each additional print ordered at the same time, you'll spend $1,080 on photography. If you submit the same prints to the three awards programs for which the building is still eligible the next year, your photography cost for each of the eight entries will be $135. If you enter the pictures in only one awards program, you'll spend $840: $750 plus $15 for each of the six prints. But your photography cost per entry will be six times higher—$840 compared to $135—and your potential for honors much less.

Cost of photography is only one of the expenses you can reduce by entering the same project in several different programs. Once drawn, floor and site plans, elevations, and sections can be photocopied or photostatted for each submission; the same general outline can serve as the basis for each different project statement.

Publicity is the third reason to enter a project in many different programs. If you receive more than one award, you're likely to be mentioned week after week in your local newspapers. Your name and pictures of your project will appear in local, regional, and national magazines, too; the exposure will attract the attention of other editors and potential clients. Arizona architect William Bruder said that after his first award-winning projects were featured in magazines and newspapers, he began to receive calls from editors of magazines that he had never approached.

Before you enter the same project in several programs at the same time, read the entry rules for all the awards programs in which you're interested. Some sponsors will not accept projects that have been featured in any regional or national publications. This means that a project honored in a state program and published in a regional magazine with limited circulation may not be eligible for some national programs. (It also means that a project featured in a manufacturer's advertisement is not eligible for some awards programs.)

If the programs you want to enter have no such restrictions, jot down all of your projects and the programs for which they're eligible. To figure out how many of these programs you can afford to enter, check the entry fees and the cost of assembling an entry: the binder, the photographs, the plans that must be redrawn. Remember that there will be additional expenses if you win; you may have to prepare display boards or submit slides for an exhibition, and you probably will have to pay your own way to the awards presentation.

Rank the awards programs by their importance to you, their prestige, the publicity they offer, their cost, and the number of years your project will be eligible for each program. When you must decide which of two equally prestigious programs to enter, choose the one for which your project is only eligible this year.

ALLOW YOURSELF ENOUGH TIME

As you consider the list of awards programs that you would like to enter, compare the program deadlines and your calendar. After you've marked off holidays, vacations, business trips, and meetings, circle the deadlines for requesting entry forms, the days your photographer is free, and the deadlines for submitting entries. Now think about when the project is scheduled to be ready for photography; allow an extra week

Program	Project to Enter	Entry Deadline	Submission Due
BD&C Young Professional	office building	none	June 8
Owens-Corning Energy Conservation	office building	none	Aug. 15
Library	Altoona branch	Nov. 25	Jan. 6
Red Cedar Shingle & Handsplit Shake Bureau Program	Wilson house	June 8	July 13

FIGURE **9-2**   SCHEDULE FOR ENTERING AWARDS PROGRAMS

for last-minute work and poor weather and circle this date on your calendar. Estimate how many days you'll need to outline and write the project statement, to draw the site and floor plans, and to select, order, and receive prints from the photographer. You'll also need to obtain your client's permission, preferably in writing. Add another week for shipping the entry to the program sponsors. Use a chart like Figure 9-2 to list the programs you would like to enter, their deadlines, the projects that are eligible, and the work that you've done on your entries. Set deadlines for your own work and check them frequently to make sure that your submission will be ready on time.

If you decide to prepare an entry just weeks before the deadline, recognize the problems you may encounter and the tension a last-minute entry will cause in your office. Want an example? Let's suppose this is November 14; after two weeks of searching, you've finally unearthed the entry rules for a residential design awards program that you would like to enter. The deadline for submitting entries is December 15.

	Photography		Text		Plans	Awards
Commissioned	Proofs	Prints	Rough	Finish		Announced
March 15	Apr. 15	Apr. 20	Apr. 5			September
"	"	"	"		Being redrawn	October
						after January
March 15	Apr. 5				Finished	September

You want to submit information and photographs of the model home you've designed. The house construction is completed, but there's a mound of scrap lumber on the lot. Your client, a builder with a small crew, doesn't plan to landscape the yard until spring; his interior designer has ordered the furnishings, but most of them have been delayed by a truckers' strike. You can't discuss the program with the builder anyway, because he left this afternoon for two weeks in Hawaii. You've never commissioned a photographer, but several of your friends have recommended someone. He's out of town on another job, but his answering service assures you he'll call when he returns next week. You spend the weekend redrawing the floor plan and listing the points you want to make in your project statement.

A week later, you're still trying to find someone to clean up the mess on the site; your client is still in Hawaii; and the furniture for the house is still in a truck somewhere. The photographer has called you and made an appointment to show you his portfolio the day before Thanksgiving. He's not exactly what you're looking for, but he says that he can work with the empty rooms and he's free the entire first week of December. After spending most of your holiday weekend struggling with the sections and your project statement, you wake up to the season's first snowfall, with the storm closing the airport and many roads. Tuesday your client's back in town, but he's so busy he's not returning calls. The scrap lumber's still on the house lot, and the furniture hasn't arrived. But the weatherman is predicting sunshine for the end of the week; the photographer gives you a list of props to bring and tells you to call him early Thursday. Wednesday night you feel feverish, and when you call the photographer the next morning, you can barely whisper. But he's ready to tackle the job, so an hour later you're helping him unpack tripods and lamps in the house. You've done the inside and moved out to try a close-up of the entry court when a truck pulls up in front of the house; it's the couch and dining room set. After you've convinced the driver to move his truck and unload in a few hours, you and the photographer finish the

job. You head home to your aspirin and your bed; it's Sunday
before you remember that the drawings haven't been photostatted, the project statement hasn't been typed, and you
need a binder in which to submit your entry. Monday the
photographer brings in the proofs and you hurriedly select
the prints you need; between running errands and proofreading the project statement, you open four days' mail and
return telephone calls. Your client finally calls and tells you
the awards program sounds great. Your prints don't come on
Wednesday as the photographer promised; he's caught your
cold, but he says the pictures will be in your office Thursday.
He drops them off at 4:45 P.M. Thursday, so you spend Friday
morning assembling the entry and checking on delivery services. At 2 P.M., the overnight air freight service picks up the
package; for a $20 charge, it'll deliver your binder to the
awards program sponsors on Monday morning, December 15.

WHAT WILL AN ENTRY COST YOU?

Last-minute entries can be very expensive; you may have to
pay for rush orders at the photographer's, air freight delivery
services, and overtime in your own office to prepare the drawings and text. Even with careful planning, some expenses
cannot be avoided. Although some awards programs entry
forms clearly state that professional photography is not required, you'll need good pictures to compete with the other
entries. "If you're going to invest your time and money in a
submittal, invest in good photography," cautions Franklin C.
Welch, who directs the Red Cedar Shingle & Handsplit Shake
Bureau's architectural awards program. "Bad photography
can defeat the whole effort." Unless you have the skill and
time to take fine pictures, hire an experienced photographer.
Estimate between $500 and $1,000 for an architectural photographer's fee and for travel and film expenses and print fees.

   Some awards program sponsors charge entry fees of as
much as $100; others only ask you to send a stamped, self-
addressed envelope for the return of your materials. Some

awards program sponsors send you entry binders; others recommend binders like the FUL-VU books made by Cooks,
Inc. These binders and others like them are available for $10
to $25 at most office supply stores. Shipping charges may
add another $25 to the cost of your entry. Many program
sponsors suggest that you submit entries by registered mail;
insure the package for the value of the photographs. If you
cannot mail the entry a week or more before the deadline, use
Express Mail or one of the guaranteed next-day delivery services like Federal Express. Be sure that the service you use
delivers directly to the program sponsor's office; awards program directors will not drive to air freight terminals to pick
up your package. Put the award program street address on the
package; freight services do not deliver to post office boxes.

YOUR SUBMISSION

Before you commission the photographer or order the entry
binder, read the entry rules carefully. If you have any questions about your eligibility for the awards program, call or
write the program director immediately; don't wait until two
weeks before the deadline, when the program sponsors will be
busy filing the first entries and planning the judging session.

Project Statement

Some awards programs limit your comments about the project to 250 words; others allow you ten typewritten pages.
Regardless of the limit, remember that shorter is better.
Judges may have more than a hundred entries to study every
day of the jury session; they don't have the time to read long
statements.

Outlining a project statement is just like planning a letter or presentation to a prospective client. You're "selling"
your project to the jurors just as you would your services to a
client. So start your project statement with the points that
are most important to the jurors. For an idea of what to men-

tion, see the entry form; it will describe the kinds of projects or services that are recognized by the program awards. Check the news stories on previous award recipients too. Make your points in short, easy-to-read sentences that jurors can skim. Clearly state the problems you were presented and the solutions you devised. As you read over your rough draft, replace generalizations and theory with specifics; eliminate jargon and slang. As you review a sentence, ask yourself if it's too long. Is it confusing? Is it padded with impressive-sounding words straight from your thesaurus?

Before you type the statement, check the accuracy of every statement, especially the dates and dollar figures. If the awards program requires anonymity, make sure that your firm name is not mentioned in the text. For the statement that goes in the entry binder, use the sheets provided by the program sponsors or light-colored, opaque paper. Type with a new, dark ribbon and the largest type available. If your text is short, use one-and-one-half or double spacing; the statement will be easier to read.

Art and Photographs

Because most large drawings of site and floor plans will be difficult to read if they're reduced to the $8\frac{1}{2} \times 11$-inch sheets required in entry binders, redraw the plans. Have them photostatted so you can submit photostats or photocopies in the binder.

To assemble your submittal, lay all of the material that you plan to use on a large table. Arrange and rearrange the art, photos, and statement until you're satisfied that you have the most dramatic presentation of your project. If possible, use all horizontal or all vertical pictures so that the jurors do not have to turn the binder several times as they study the pictures. Once you've assembled your entry, photocopy each page for your files.

If you include slides in your entry, insert them in a page of slide-size pockets that can be added to the three-ring binder or slipped inside the clear sleeves of a bound entry book. If you tape the slides to cardboard, the jurors probably won't even look at the pictures. Label all slides and photographs with the project name or number that you've used in the project statement and on the entry form. Do not indicate your name or the firm name on anything but the concealed identification form.

Concealed Identification

Remember that inscriptions for awards certificates and plaques are often taken directly from the information that you provide on concealed identification forms. The awards program director may write the press releases using this information, too. Check the accuracy of the firm names that you list; if your client has requested anonymity, don't add his or her name to this information sheet.

Copyright

Because many awards program sponsors use entry materials in publications, advertisements, magazine stories, and with press releases, the pictures you submit should be free of copyright restrictions. If your photographer insists on being paid if your entry materials are published in magazines or ads, point this out to the program sponsors. Do not use pictures taken by a professional photographer in an entry without discussing rights with the photographer; otherwise you may find yourself in the middle of a lawsuit.

THE REWARDS

If a project you enter in an awards program is honored, you may receive a certificate, an award symbol, or a trip to the awards presentation. You may be featured in magazine stories and in advertisements and brochures published by the awards program sponsors. You may even receive cash. Architects who are honored with the R. S. Reynolds Memorial

Awards receive $25,000 honorariums as well as aluminum sculptures and publicity.

You don't have to be a winner to benefit from entering an awards program, however. In many programs, every entry is studied for its potential as a news story or an illustration for an advertisement. Some entries are submitted to magazine editors; others are published in corporate magazines. For example, at the Red Cedar Shingle & Handsplit Shake Bureau, the awards program director carefully reads each entry; he features many of them in *Mallet & Froe*, the cedar bureau publication. For many years at the American Plywood Association, winners of the Plywood Design Awards program were pictured in a multi-page ad. The last page of the ad was always devoted to small pictures of construction details; most of these pictures came from entries that had not received awards. The editors at *Professional Builder*, the plywood program cosponsor, reviewed most of the entries for news value. One year, the magazine devoted ten pages to pictures of the award-winning buildings and another four pages in the same issue to stories on several other entries.

Getting to know the editors and publicists who run awards programs is another of the benefits of entering the programs. Even if your project is not selected for an award, an advertisement, a product catalog, or a feature story, an awards program director who is impressed with your work will call you when he or she is researching a story or planning an ad. The director may also give your name and a description of your projects to other editors and publicists.

MARKETING WITH AWARDS

The most valuable award is the one that helps you market yourself. How can you tell if an award will help you market yourself? Start with publicity: How much does the award offer? Entry forms often make vague references to national publicity and exhibits at conventions and trade shows; when you learn that you've received an award, ask the awards pro-

gram director about press releases, photographs, magazine
features, advertisements, brochures, exhibits, and award presentations. Will the press releases be sent to local newspapers
and to regional and national magazines? Will magazine
editors be offered information for feature stories? Will your
project be pictured in an advertisement or a brochure announcing the award recipients? Will the awards be presented
at a national convention or in your hometown? Will press
releases and photographs of the awards presentation be sent
to local newspapers?

Ask the awards program director or publicity coordinator how you can help. Offer to provide a list (with addresses and telephone numbers) of the newspapers and magazines to which you would like press releases mailed. If you're
asked to check a press release for accuracy, read it as soon as
you receive it, clearly mark any necessary corrections . . . and
resist the temptation to rewrite it. If advertisements or
brochures will be printed, ask how many free copies you'll
receive and how you can order in quantity. (Extra copies of
printed materials are often available at very low cost if you
order before they are printed.)

Use the publicity that follows the presentation of an
award just as you would use other press coverage. Collect
clippings of the newspaper stories and tear sheets or reprints
of the magazine features and advertisements. Mail these to
your clients and consultants with personal notes about the
award. Remember everyone who was involved with the project; for example, if you receive a design award, call or write
the builder, the contractor and subcontractors, the interior
designer and the landscape architect, the engineers, the suppliers, and the photographer who helped you prepare your
entry. Post the clippings and reprints in your office and send
copies of them with the brochures that you send to potential
clients.

At the awards presentation, ask the awards program
director for introductions to editors and publicists. If the
awards are presented at a large national or regional convention, you'll see reporters, editors, and representatives of

manufacturers' marketing staffs at the lectures, in the hospitality and exhibit rooms, and at other awards presentations. Ask the manufacturers' reps if their firms promote the work of people like yourself who use their materials; tell the editors about your other projects and about special problems that they might find newsworthy. Follow up these meetings with friendly notes; for some examples, see Chapter 3.

If the award is presented in your hometown, ask your client to attend the presentation. Arrange for the awards program director to present the client with a duplicate certificate. If the award is for a project in your community, ask the awards program director if you can invite the local editors to the presentation.

Officially hang or unveil the award in your reception or conference area at a party for your clients, your consultants, your staff, and the local press. Banner the top of your existing ads with the name of the award or a picture of the award symbol; apply medal-style self-adhesive seals with the name of the award to the sales literature that you've already had printed. Add phrases like "award-winning," "honored in the . . ." and "recognized by the . . ." to your firm and project descriptions. Make up title slides with excerpts from the jury comment for your slide presentations. Add the full name of the award and the year you received it to your list of honors; add the titles of stories resulting from the award to your record of published projects. And, of course, rewrite your résumé to include the award.

WHAT CONTESTS SHOULD YOU ENTER?

Forget the lottery, the sweepstakes, and the VFW raffle. The contests you should be entering don't promise something for nothing; to win, you have to demonstrate skill and talent. The most valuable contests not only require you to demonstrate your skill, they publicize it to your potential customers. For example, if you run a kennel, families are your most likely customers. Your prize-winning entry in the "Prettiest Pet" contest sponsored by a women's magazine will win you a ribbon—and at least a short story in a magazine read by hundreds of women in your own town.

How do you find contests like these? You find them the same way you learn about awards programs. Read the stories and the advertisements in the magazines and newspapers that are published for your potential customers and for amateurs with interests like your professional skill. If you're a cabinetmaker, watch handyman magazines for woodworking and carpentry contests; if you sell cookware or run a catering service, watch women's magazines and gourmet cooking journals for cooking contests. Most county and state fairs have contests, too: some are for grange members, some for 4-H'ers, and others for the general public. You'll find other contests at some local festivals, too.

WHY ENTER CONTESTS?

Why should you enter contests? Obviously, the *Woman's Day* readers in Tarzana, California, and Trenton, New Jersey, may enjoy a story about your prize-winning pups, but they're not likely to travel to Minneapolis for the pick of your next litter. And just because you design a table that takes first prize in *Popular Science*'s plywood project contest, you won't have every furniture manufacturer from North Carolina west knocking on your door. What you will have is a certificate or a ribbon, a plaque or a trophy, and a few inquiries from the *Woman's Day* or *Popular Science* readers in your area. You may have a prize, too; a check for $25 or $25,000, a collection of how-to books, a microwave oven—maybe even a trip around the world or a complete kitchen remodeling. With any contest, you will also have publicity that you can use in a related business—and some very valuable contacts.

For example, if you run a kennel, you can send a copy of the story to the pet columnist of your local paper; you can pin up a tear sheet on your veterinarian's waiting room bulletin board; and you can send reprints to your regular customers.

Post a copy of the story in your own office and send one to the photographer who took the pictures you entered. If you're the furniture designer, you can send a press release and photo of your table to the "home" section editors of your local papers; send reprints of the magazine feature and personal letters to furniture manufacturers and to the "workshop" editors of women's magazines that buy designs. Invite the interior designers in your area to a party celebrating the prize, too.

Get to know the editors and publicists who run the contests for magazines and manufacturers. When you win a contest, express your delight to the contest coordinator with a note like this:

> Your note announcing my red ribbon in the "Rice to Riches" cooking contest arrived yesterday. What a pleasant surprise! I look forward to seeing the recipe in your new cookbook; make sure my name is on the top of your mailing list!

Write a follow-up note when your project is published in a magazine or book, too. For example, suppose your winning rice dish is featured in a women's magazine. Write a note like this to the editor whose name appears on the story or to the head of the cooking department:

> I'm so pleased with the budget meals feature in your October 18 issue. How exciting to see my Razzle-Dazzle Rice pictured!
>
> I'm still working on low-cost meals; if you'd like a sample, stop in on your next visit to the Midwest.

The editors and publicists may call you when they're planning trips to your area—or when they need more suggestions for cost-cutting meals. Some of them will never call you, but they'll remember your name when you call them to propose another story or when you want the name of an editor in another department. For example, suppose you're an architect who talked to *Popular Science* Reader Activities Editor Alfred Lees once or twice after you won the grand prize in the magazine's Plywood Project Contest. From reading *Popular Science*, you know Lees runs the magazine's leisure home series, so when you design an unusual vacation cabin, it's easy to suggest that he look at your drawings.

HOW TO WIN A CONTEST

How do you win a contest? Read the rules—all of them. And follow them; don't expect the judges to make exceptions for you. Be original, but not outrageous; make your entry something other people will want to make or build or wear and make your entry something other people *can* make or build or sew, too; use inexpensive, readily available ingredients or materials, and make the instructions easy to understand.

10

ADVERTISING

The stories about you and your firm that are published in newspapers and magazines are news; you don't pay for the publicity. Advertisements are different; you decide what you want to say, you provide the pictures, and you pay for the portion of a page or the time your advertisement requires. That's not the only difference. News stories are edited; they're rewritten, shortened, or discarded, depending on what the editor needs. Advertisements aren't edited; they're printed exactly when and how you specify.

What's the first step in planning an advertising campaign? How do you select an advertising agency? How do you design and write ads without an agency? How can you tell how many potential customers read your ad? You'll find the answers here. Intended as an introduction to advertising, this chapter also provides details on the print ads many small businesses use. For information on direct mail, see Chapter 11. For details on radio and television commercials, see the publications listed in Appendix A.

SHOULD YOU ADVERTISE?

That depends on what you're trying to do. Besides promoting your products, advertising can generate public support; the people in your community may help you fight for a variance from environmental control standards or against a sales tax increase. You can also use advertising to motivate your employees and to recruit new ones; you can communicate to your competitors; and you can sometimes raise your stock price and improve the sales of your bonds.

Whether advertising improves your sales and helps you cut your selling costs depends on your business. Advertising isn't necessary for some products and services—and it's essential for others. Like publicity, premiums, price reductions, samples, and a sales representative's calls, an advertisement is one of the many marketing tools you can use. It's not a substitute for any of the others, especially the sales call. Most advertisements are not designed to sell products. Their job is to sell you—to make people aware of you and to create a favorable image for you. With this introduction, you sell the product.

The best ad—the one that really helps you sell—is designed and written to work with press releases, product catalogs, displays, demonstrations, samples, and the sales calls; together they provide a continuous flow of information about your products to potential customers. Because every marketing program takes time to affect how people buy, use the same advertising theme or campaign until marketing conditions change so much that you need a different strategy.

161

An ad can be a couple of lines in the newspaper's classified section or the front inside cover of a magazine; it can be a jingle on the radio or a thirty-second "slice of life" on television. It can be a billboard, a readerboard, a sandwich board, or the banner trailing a low-flying plane. An ad can be a two-inch square in the Yellow Pages, a poster, a postcard, or a computer-personalized letter. The most valuable advertising is word-of-mouth—what your satisfied customers tell their friends, neighbors, and co-workers about you and the work you do.

BEFORE YOU PLAN AN AD

Before you jot down a word of copy or read a rate card, draw a mental picture of the people you're trying to reach. Who are they? Are they men or women, old or young, single or married, professionals, craftspeople, or academics? What's more important to them: cost, convenience, quality, service, a broad product line, or a guarantee? Where are these potential customers? Are they concentrated in large industrial cities or in small towns in rural areas? Do they know who you are and what you sell?

Now think about what you're trying to sell. Is it something that people know they need, like detergent? Or is it a complicated new product that people don't understand? If your product is new, you'll probably have to use your ads to tell people what you're selling and why they need it. If you've got several competitors, tell people why your product's better. If you're selling something that's been on the market for years, try case histories. They will show who uses your product, why they like it, and what it does for them.

Sometimes your customers don't need much information—your name, address, telephone number, and hours are enough. More often, they want details; they want to know how the product operates, what it's made of, how much it costs, what options are available, where they can order it, and when it will be delivered. For other products, your customers will want pictures, not words; they want to see what the product looks like and how it is used.

WHAT KIND OF AD?

Once you know whom you're trying to reach and what kind of information these people want, you'll have a better idea of what kind of ad to run and what it should say and show. For short messages, try a picture and a few words on a billboard; hire a skywriter to scrawl your brand name in the sky above a county fair or local festival. If your product is easy to understand and you want to reach people who work, ask a radio station to read your thirty-second commercial during the morning and evening commuting hours. To reach children, film a commercial in your local television station's studio and have it aired every Saturday morning between cartoons. To illustrate the glamour of new fall fashions, buy a page in the Sunday magazine and run a charcoal sketch of a chic, slender woman.

What's the best way to present your message? Think about the people whom you are trying to reach and what you need to say. Check what's available in your area and take a look at your advertising budget. Television reaches nearly every home; with it, you can demonstrate how your products look, sound, and work. You can almost make people feel and taste them, too. Because different programs appeal to different people, you can direct your commercials to those who are most likely to buy your products. Television is expensive, however; commercials are expensive to make and air time is costly. Because there are so many other commercials, you'll have difficulty attracting attention to yours. People tune out commercials and walk away from them, too. Another problem: there are very few programs for people who don't speak English. Radio is much less expensive, both in production and air time. You can reach different racial and ethnic groups with special programs and stations. The radio ads, however, won't have the visual appeal of television, and you will still have to compete with the many other commercials for people's attention. With both radio and television, you're limited to very short ads; the most time you'll have is a minute.

When you advertise in daily newspapers, the cost is usually low and you have lots of flexibility; you can insert or stop an ad within hours of the press run. You can reach well-educated people in a specific geographic area. With a newspaper ad, you have another advantage; the authority of the news columns rubs off on your ad, giving it a credibility it might not otherwise have. And you'll have space for lengthy explanations or bold poster-style graphics. With special sections like "weekend living" or "sports," you can reach special groups. Suburban papers, usually concentrated in affluent communities, offer you very specific geographic coverage. The cost of an ad in a suburban weekly is often low, but sometimes so are the readership and the editorial quality. Some city magazines are slick books with color features and provocative articles; others are nothing more than local entertainment guides. Before you run an ad, read the publication carefully and check the circulation figures.

Trade publications go to well-defined groups of professionals or business people who want information. The cost of an ad varies according to the nature of the publication and its circulation; a color page can cost you several hundred dollars in one trade journal and several thousand in another. Many trade publications offer reader service numbers; as people read the magazine, they can mark the numbers representing companies from which they would like more information. From the lists of people who ask about your products, you can measure the response to your ad, but you'll wait a month or more after the ad appears to get the lists from the magazine. The editorial quality of trade journals is inconsistent, too; some are very good and others are just collections of ads and product publicity photographs.

With direct mail, you can segment your audience according to profession, industry, size of business, or geographic location; you can time mailings to your convenience and needs; and you can describe complicated products and services. Direct mail can be expensive, however, even with third-class bulk rate postage. And to many people, direct mail smacks of "junk mail."

Billboards and signs let you reach people in specific neighborhoods; they're inexpensive, they have impact, and they have visibility. Use them if you're selling inexpensive products that appeal to most people. You can't segment your audience—and you can't say more than a few words. With transit cards—the posters in buses, subways, and commuter trains—you're also limited to a very simple message and particular geographic areas. Sometimes you're limited to a low-income audience. With an ad in the Yellow Pages, a city directory, or a professional catalog, you'll reach people in the specific town or industry you serve. You'll also reach them when they're ready to buy.

PLANNING THE AD

To produce an ad, you may not have to do anything more complicated than have your name, address, and local prices typeset or taped. Manufacturers and retailers who distribute products across a region or the country often produce newspaper and magazine ads and television and radio commercials; the names of local dealers are listed at the bottom of print ads or at the end of broadcast commercials. Other manufacturers will send you photographs and drawings that you can cut out and paste onto your ads or scripts that you can have taped for radio commercials. The manufacturers who provide these materials usually also pay part of the cost of placing the ad. For example, if you run an ad showing the new Gant shirts available in your menswear store, Gant Shirtmakers may pay for as much as fifty percent of the space. To find out what cooperative advertising deals your suppliers offer, talk to the sales representatives who call on you. Negotiate for the best co-op deal possible; manufacturers usually give good customers larger co-op allowances.

You can also add your name to the standard advertisements provided by a newspaper. Most papers have clip books of ads, headlines, and art; you can run your name at the bottom of a preprinted New Year's greeting or combine a stock headline and picture with your copy for a Valentine's Day or back-to-school special. Having an ad designed with stock materials is quick and inexpensive; you don't have to pay for special drawings or hand-lettered headlines.

And you can have your firm listed on the large ads most newspapers publish to celebrate events like Pioneer Day, 4-H Week, and Law Day. The newspaper staff designs the ad, often using standard art, and divides the cost of the space among the businesses listed. These ads are goodwill gestures; they don't allow you to say anything about your business. However, they do show you're involved in the community; in some small towns, not adding your name to these ads is as serious an error as not attending Chamber of Commerce meetings, high school basketball games, or Sunday school picnics.

When you want an advertisement designed especially for you, ask the newspaper, magazine, or broadcast station staff for help; hire an advertising agency; or do the design, writing, and typesetting yourself. When you're working with the advertising staff of a publication or a station, go in with an idea of what you want. For a print ad, make a few small pencil sketches and type a draft of your copy. For a commercial, put together a rough script or the information that you would like a disc jockey to incorporate into his or her patter. If you would rather work with an agency, look for one that handles products like yours; if you offer legal services or high quality industrial grinding wheels, you may not want to work with an agency that films commercials for hair coloring and hamburgers. To find an agency, ask the business people you know for the names of the firms that handle their advertising. Watch the business page of your newspaper; it may list the new agencies that are opening and the accounts that are changing agencies. When you call an agency to ask for a presentation, briefly describe your product and the ads you want to run.

When you're meeting with advertising people, think about whether or not you would be comfortable working with them. Are they so young and unconventional that they irritate or intimidate you? Do they have the imagination and originality to create the ads you need? Do the people seem to value you and your ideas—or will they soon be telling you that your account is not worth their time? (If you only plan a few ads, don't be surprised if the account executive at a large agency tactfully suggests that you try a smaller firm. Be grateful for this honesty and ask him or her to recommend firms or free-lancers you should contact.)

When you discuss your advertising program with people from different agencies, tell them as much as you can about your product and its uses; about your customers and the people you would like to make your customers; about your sales, broken down by product, season, and customer group; and about your promotion budget. Explain your goals, too. Do you want your business to grow? How much? How fast? Do you want new customers—or do you want to sell your current customers more?

Don't hesitate to talk about money. Ask how the agency charges and how much certain programs may cost you. Be honest about your budget; point out the cash flow problems that may force you to reduce or eliminate advertising.

DESIGNING AN AD YOURSELF

If you're designing a print ad yourself, start with these two rules: make the ad organized, so that it's easy to read, and make it interesting, so that people want to read it. To make an ad easy to read, organize the different elements, the lines and planes of type and art. Try making one picture or one headline the focal point; or suggest a curve that the eye naturally follows through the ad. Use lines or borders to pull the eye to the most important point. Keep the graphics simple; limit yourself to three styles of type, counting your logo as one. If you're looking for a classic type style, try one with serifs, the small lines that finish the longer strokes of a letter. For a clean, modern look, use sans serif type.

To make an ad interesting, consider an off-center design. Use wide margins for elegance. Try a photograph, a drawing, or symbols. An illustration that supports the ad's content does several jobs: it generally attracts attention to the ad, and it screens your readers by showing what the ad is promoting and so attracting those who have the means and desire to buy. It tells part of your story and it reinforces the message in your headline and copy. A border can hold the ad together visually and separate it from other material on the same page; it also attracts attention to the ad or works with the logo that identifies your company or product name. If your ad will be all type, select attractive typefaces that are easy to read and use lots of white space; with a strong headline, you can create a very effective ad.

You may want a little color—one letter of your name printed in red or one part of your drawing outlined in blue. You may want full (often called four) color; or you may prefer black and white. Color doesn't necessarily make an ad better, especially if your ad will appear in a publication with mediocre color reproduction. Black and white is much less expensive, and it can be very dramatic.

Try several designs; rough them out on scraps of paper with a soft lead pencil. When you find an idea you like, make your sketch a little larger. Lightly pencil in the headlines so that you can estimate how many letters you'll have. If you're having the type set, a typesetter can help you select a typeface and size; if you're using dry transfer letters, stencils, or hand lettering, estimate how many letters you'll be able to use on each line. If you letter your headlines and text on a separate sheet of heavy white paper, you can cut out the words and rubber cement them to the mechanical. Misspelled or poorly lettered words can then be easily replaced.

Remember:

allow at least $\frac{5}{16}$ of an inch as a gutter between two
  columns of type;
allow more space between lines than between
  letters;

ragged right copy (justified on the left, but not on the right) is the easiest to read and to print; and ragged left copy is the hardest to read.

WRITING THE COPY

When you pick up your pencil, remember that this is advertising, not journalism. Forget about objectivity; be honest, but make your product sound terrific. Instead of telling people how good your product is, tell them how it'll save them time and money and make them happier and more comfortable. Tell them how your product will solve their problems. Try strong, exciting, active verbs like "save," "win," "create," and "discover." When you use adjectives, be as specific as you can; when you say "quick," say how quick. When you say "flavorful," say what it tastes like. When you say "feels good," tell your readers how good. Want an example of excellent copy? Look at this: "Raid kills bugs dead." As John E. O'Toole of the advertising agency Foote Cone & Belding has pointed out, that's much stronger than "Bugs are made lifeless by Raid." (It's shorter, too, and it's easier to read.)

As you write, pretend you're the salesperson talking to a potential customer. What's the most important thing you could tell a customer about this product? What words would you use? Put these into writing. Writing advertising copy isn't hard if you keep reminding yourself of the person you're trying to talk to—but remember you won't have a chance to answer questions or correct misimpressions.

Make one major point; that's probably all your reader has time for. And remember that the first words you write are the most important; many of the people you're trying to reach will quit reading after the first ten, twenty-five, or fifty words. Avoid jokes that steal attention from the theme of the ad, avoid hackneyed phrases, and avoid exaggeration. Keep your copy short, especially if you run frequent ads reminding people to buy a familiar, inexpensive product. Provide more information if you're trying to tell people about a new or complex product or if you're trying to reassure them about an expensive or high-risk purchase. In the copy, offer your reader something. Include a coupon, a postcard, or a reader service number in your ad, so that the reader can write for a brochure or a sample; print a cents-off coupon or tell where he or she can write for a refund. Publish a toll-free number or the names of your local sales representatives so that customers can call for more information or a demonstration. You'll motivate people to do something—and you'll give yourself a means of measuring how many potential customers read your ad. Code your coupons or postcards by the magazines in which they appear; for example, the coupon that appears in the July issue of *Better Homes and Gardens* might tell readers to write Dept. BHG-7 at your address.

If you would like help with your design or writing, hire a graphic artist or a copywriter. For more suggestions on selecting someone to help you, see Chapter 11.

GETTING THE AD PUBLISHED

Before you deliver or mail your ad to a publication, have the black-and-white pictures converted to screen prints. (Check with the newspaper; its staff may be willing to make the screen prints.) When a picture is screened, its black, white, and gray tones are reduced to dots; because presses do not print gray, each dot is either black or white. The finer the screen used (and the higher the screen number), the smaller the dots. On a good press, smaller dots mean sharper pictures; on a poor press, the dots will all run together. For the best reproduction of pictures in magazines and newspapers, use the screen recommended by the publisher; you can call the publication for this or check *Standard Rate & Data Services*, a multi-volume monthly catalog available in many public libraries. Take color art to a quality printer to have separations made; for a full-color ad, you'll need red, yellow, blue, and black separations—one for each time the page goes through the press.

If your mechanical (the sheet on which the ad is pasted

up) is a combination of many different pieces of type and art, or if you're sending a black-and-white ad to several publications, have the mechanical photostatted. This will give you a sharp image that will reproduce well—and you won't have to worry about a word or a drawing falling off the mechanical before the publication is printed. Send a photostat to each magazine and newspaper that will publish the ad. With a photostat, you also can change the size of the ad; you or the publication staff can have the ad reduced or enlarged to fit a particular column width or page size.

You can submit an ad to a publication's advertising department or office; you'll find the addresses of a magazine's advertising offices on the masthead or contents page. Newspapers list their offices in the telephone book; larger papers have advertising salespeople who will pick up your ads. You can also submit ads to the services that represent newspapers; for example, if you'd like to run an ad in several of Washington state's weekly papers, you can send your ad to the Seattle office of the Washington Newspaper Publishers' Association. It will distribute copies of the ad to the papers that you've specified. You'll find the names of publications' representatives in the *Editor & Publisher International Year Book* and in *Standard Rate & Data Service*.

HOW MUCH WILL AN AD COST?

How much you spend on advertising depends on many factors: the size of your ad, how often you run it, whether you use color, the publications you use, and who designs and produces the ad. The cost of your advertising program also depends on whether you favor "reach" or "frequency." Reach (sometimes called cumulative audience, net reach, or unduplicated reach) is defined as the number of people who are reached at least once by your ad. For the greatest reach, you would advertise in several publications, each with a different group of readers. Because you would be advertising in so many different publications, you might be able to afford only one or two ads in each one during a year. If you prefer to reach a smaller group more frequently, you might run an ad in every issue of one magazine that is read by people whom you consider to be potential customers. Because magazines offer discount rates to regular advertisers, you might spend less even though you're running more ads.

Another way to save money: Run your ad only in certain editions of magazines and newspapers. Major metropolitan papers are printed with different editions for each part of the city or suburb; magazines publish different editions for regions or professional groups. For information on the special editions and rates, consult *Editor & Publisher* and *Standard Rate & Data Service*. Most newspapers quote their rates in lines; fourteen lines of agate type equals one column inch. A column inch, a standard newspaper unit of measure, is one vertical inch of the column, regardless of the column's width. Magazines usually quote their rates by pages except for sections like the classified, where small ads are available.

HOW MUCH SHOULD YOU SPEND?

How much should you spend on advertising? There's no magic number. Some marketing consultants recommend a percentage of sales; they say, for example, that a builder should spend one or two percent of his or her sales revenue on advertising. If you're going to use an advertising/sales ratio as your rule of thumb, try spending a percentage of what you hope to make. Then you won't be advertising on the basis of past sales; when you come out of a bad year, your advertising budget will reflect optimism, not the poor sales of the year before.

What you should spend is often determined by your competitors. How much you spend is not determined by how much they spend, but how strong they are and how good their entire marketing programs are. Can you steal a competitor's business with larger ads or more commercials? Probably not. Remember that advertising is only one of your marketing tools—and it may not be the most important one.

BEFORE AN AD IS PUBLISHED

Before your advertisement is published, prepare for the inquiries you expect. If the ad offers a publication, make sure that it has been printed and is ready to mail. (If you're producing a new product catalog or brochure, have it designed by whoever designs your ad; you'll have two complementary pieces and you may save some money, especially if you're using color.) If the ad offers samples, have them boxed and ready to be labeled. If you're publishing a toll-free number, make sure that it's operating. Prepare your sales representatives, distributors, dealers, and employees for the questions that they may be asked, too. Send them copies of the ads, show them the commercials, and give them lists of the media in which the ads will appear.

Decide how you're going to measure the response to the ad; if you've included a coded coupon, record how many coupons with each code are returned so that you will know which publication brought the most responses. When people telephone for more information, have your receptionist or operator ask the callers where they read about your product. Record how many inquiries result from the ad each day, each week, or each month. Keep track of how many of these inquiries result in sales.

For your most important dealers or customers, ask the magazine publisher for copies of the first issues printed; many publishers will attach cover letters to the issues and mail them for you. This is a particularly valuable marketing tool when the ad includes a case history about one of your customers or a testimonial from one of them.

WHAT TO EXPECT FROM AN AD

No one can predict what your ad will bring. Your phone may start to ring as soon as the newspaper's delivered—or you may not have a call for a week. Within days after a magazine is printed, you may have bags of mail—or just a few inquiries. If you're disappointed about the response to an ad that you have run, reread the first page of this chapter; remember that a good ad is only one part of a marketing program. Be realistic; don't expect immediate results.

Prospective customers may have to see several of your ads before they even become aware of your product; they may wait weeks, months, or years before they decide to try it. Marketing experts suggest that there are several steps between becoming aware of a product and buying it regularly. Your ads help move prospective customers from one step to another—from awareness to information-gathering to preferring your product to the others on the market. After you've introduced a product, the next step is convincing the customer to try it. Then there's the trial purchase and finally the continued purchase and use. Sometimes this process works very fast; when you see a point-of-purchase display at a supermarket register, you may move from awareness to trial purchase within seconds. When a product is more expensive or complicated or when it's something that you don't need very often, the process takes much longer.

FOLLOW UP!

When people call or write you for more information, send them brochures, product catalogs, or samples; invite them to demonstrations and send their names to sales representatives. Send lists of these prospective customers to your dealers, distributors, and brokers, too. If you receive inquiries from people in an area that you don't serve, reply with a polite form letter that refers them to companies in their city. Use reprints of your ad in sales presentations and for a direct mail program. These reprints are available from the advertising agency that produces your ads or from the magazine in which the ad appears. When you place an ad with a magazine, ask about the reprint service. Some magazines make a business of selling reprints, and they'll quote you prices and minimum order quantities. Other magazines will have the reprints done by local printers as a service to you.

Usually you'll pay the printing cost plus a ten or fifteen percent markup to cover handling. You can order reprints of just your ad or of your ad inside a folder with the magazine cover on the front. Some magazines (*Better Homes and Gardens* is one example) sell folders with a standard cover photograph; you can order any quantity for a few cents each and have your ad reprinted inside. Many magazines will also sell you reprints of feature stories describing your products, services, or industry. For more suggestions on using these reprints, see Chapter 3.

11

PRESENTING YOURSELF IN PRINT

Everything that represents your firm—the sign on your door, your advertisements, your business cards and brochure, your announcements and party invitations, your slide presentations, and your office itself—tells people something about you and the way you do business. Whether you're writing a speech, announcing an address change, or showing prospective clients your office and factory, you're marketing yourself and your firm. Everything you do and show can enhance—or tarnish—your image.

This chapter opens with brochures: their purpose, contents, format, and production. Although written primarily for professionals, this section provides suggestions for anyone who works with printers, graphic designers, and copywriters. You'll find the comments on writing your own copy helpful whether you're putting together a design brochure or describing drills and bits. There are also some examples of client presentations that are less expensive and more versatile than brochures. "Setting" type without a printer, announcements, newsletters, and mailing lists are next. The chapter concludes with direct mail programs: how to buy mailing lists, how to mail through mailing houses, and how to cut postage costs.

BROCHURES FOR PROFESSIONAL FIRMS

A brochure can be a valuable marketing tool. Like a graphic designer's portfolio, a copywriter's reel, or a printer's samples, a brochure shows what kind of work a firm has done. It also should tell prospective clients what services the firm offers and something about the people with whom the clients will be working.

How much should you spend on a brochure? How should it be designed? How should you use it? All of these depend on your firm, your industry—and the way you do business. A commercial photographer's brochure may be a simple black-and-white folder or a fifty-page catalog complete with color pictures, a detailed biography, and a list of clients. The designers who specialize in hotel and restaurant interiors may produce a new eight-page envelope-size brochure every year, while the engineers who design sewage treatment plants may describe their projects on separate unnumbered pages that are used for five or ten years.

Before you decide on a format, before you even consider which projects or services to include, ask yourself these questions: Whom am I trying to reach? What do these people know about me, my firm, and my industry? Are they interested in what I have to say? Do they trust me? Do they believe my services are necessary?

Then think about what you'll tell these people. Will you provide general information about your industry? Will you explain the services you offer? Is it important to impress people with your experience and your credentials? Do you want to convince people that they need you? How you answer these questions will determine not only what you say in your brochure, but how you say it: whether services are listed or explained in detail, whether you use many pictures or a few, whether awards are listed in large type or small.

In your brochure, as in your other presentations, explain how you diagnose problems. Describe the people who will handle a client's project and list the resources that they may use. Tell whether these resources are other people in your firm, consultants, professional or trade associations, educational institutions, or testing laboratories. In the insert written for a specific firm or industry, describe problems similar to your prospective clients'. Explain in detail how you handled these. Did you finish the job on time and under budget? Then say so. Did you recommend action that has since saved your client time and money? Then say how many hours and how many dollars. In the cover letter that accompanies your brochure, tell your prospective clients exactly how you will tackle their project: outline the possible phases of the job and point out when you'll meet with them or send them reports.

BROCHURE FORMATS

A brochure can be a folder, a booklet, or a bound volume. It may have no binding at all; its pages may be inserted in envelopes, boxes, or the pockets of folders. The brochure may have pockets for letters, proposals, or reprints; it may have die cuts that hold a business card. Some brochures are designed to fit into letter-size envelopes; others must be mailed in 8 × 10-inch envelopes. Some brochures are cut from standard size sheets or paper; others are unusual sizes like 8 × 8 inches or 10 × 10 inches. They require special cutting and custom-designed envelopes.

Before you select a format, consider the impact that you would like your brochure to have. How often will you revise it? What materials will you send with it? How will your clients file it? How much can you afford for printing, packing, and mailing? An oversize brochure may have dramatic bleed pictures and elegant expanses of white space, but it will be expensive to print and mail. If it won't fit into standard file drawers, it will be difficult for clients to file. A small brochure won't be as impressive and it may be lost in deep file drawers, but it will be less expensive to print; you'll be able to revise it frequently. You can mail it in standard envelopes, eliminating the expense of special-order envelopes and reducing postage costs.

If you design and print separate data sheets on your projects, services, and staff, you can combine the sheets in any order you like. You can write more than one data sheet on each project and staff member to emphasize different challenges and skills. You can add special inserts for each prospective client. The sheets can be bound together in several ways. If the pages are drilled, either by a printer or on the three-hole punch in your office, they can be compiled in a three-ring or multi-ring binder. They can be bound with plastic or with metal spirals by a printer or with a machine that you can buy. You can also insert the sheets in a folder, envelope, or box. Remember, however, that although you may carefully assemble the data sheets in the order that you consider most logical or dramatic, your prospective client will rearrange the project descriptions as he or she studies them. This format has two other serious disadvantages: First, people are likely to be confused when they receive a box with several loose sheets of paper. And mailing a box of data sheets is expensive; to protect the box, you'll need heavy cardboard on either side of it and a large envelope or packing bag.

Brochure Design

Even if you're spending only a few hundred dollars on a simple folder, consider calling in a graphic designer. This is especially important if you have no design training or experience. A designer can help you avoid costly mistakes and produce a brochure that may be used for years with only minor revisions. A designer also can save you time and worry; besides designing your brochure, he or she will have the type set and pasted up into the mechanical that is sent to the printer. A designer will select ink colors and paper types, weights, and colors. If you need photographs taken, the designer will plan the pictures, hire the models, and supervise the photography.

Graphic designers often work for printers, for advertising and public relations agencies, and for architectural and interior design firms. Your Yellow Pages may list communications consultants, graphic consultants, and graphic artists. You also can obtain the names of designers from professional associations like the Society of Professional Graphic Artists, Women in Advertising, and Women in Design. Ask your friends and business associates who designed their stationery, their logos, their advertisements, and their brochures. Read newsletters and annual reports carefully; some list the designers and printers who produced the publications.

To save money, hire an advanced graphic design student or a free-lance designer who is establishing a new practice. To find students, call art schools or the vocational-technical schools with graphic design programs. Ask to speak to the director of the graphic design program. Most teachers will recommend current students or recent graduates; an instructor also might be interested in using your brochure as a class project. If you can wait several weeks for your design, the students may offer several suggestions at no cost to you. Many design instructors also free-lance themselves. You can get the names of other free-lance designers from the art directors of advertising agencies.

When you call designers, invite each to show you his or her portfolio. Explain that you're obtaining cost estimates from several designers. Before you meet with the designer, jot down the information that the designer will need to give you an estimate. Decide what brochure format you prefer and how many pages you think you'll need. Will the printing be in black and white or color? How many copies of the brochure will you need? When do you need them? Be ready to show the designer other brochures that you particularly like or dislike. And don't forget to show your stationery and the other printed material that might be sent with the brochure.

A designer will not start work on your project until you formally commission him or her. After you've talked to two or three designers, looked at their portfolios, and received their estimates, hire the designer who has impressed you—with a portfolio, with attitude, and with understanding of your business. If the designer does not ask you to sign a contract, write him or her to confirm your oral agreement. Ask for periodic bills so that you can monitor costs. Clarify the services you need and the date upon which the work must be completed. State whether or not you'll credit the designer on the brochure. (You may receive better work from both the designer and the printer if they know their names will be listed on the final product.)

Brochure Writing

If you will be writing your own text for the brochure, remember the suggestions at the beginning of this chapter. Think first of the people who will read this brochure. Then decide what information about your firm and your projects is most important to these people. Put these facts together in short sentences that are easy to read. Avoid boasts, generalizations, lengthy philosophical statements, and detailed histories of your business. Eliminate jargon and slang; double check the accuracy and spelling of all the names, locations, and figures you mention. Use the style manual in your dictionary to check your grammar and punctuation. Type and proofread your text carefully. For more suggestions about writing, consult *The Elements of Style* by Strunk and White, *Word Watcher's Handbook* by Phyllis Martin, *The Art of Readable Writing* by Rudolf Flesch, and the other reference books listed in Appendix A.

If you know that you cannot write the well-organized, client-oriented text you need, hire a copywriter. Finding someone who writes as you would like to can take some time; start by asking your graphic designer for recommendations.

Call small advertising and public relations agencies; they may be interested in the project. If they're not, ask them to recommend free-lance writers. Check with instructors in college advertising and journalism programs. You might even post a "help wanted" notice outside creative writing classrooms.

When you interview copywriters, ask to see samples of their work. Before you ask for cost estimates, explain approximately how many words you'll need. (A double-spaced typewritten page with $1\frac{1}{2}$-inch margins has about 300 words.) List the kinds of projects that must be described. If a student or inexperienced writer cannot provide a cost estimate, be prepared to suggest a figure. This might be as little as $50 for 1,000 words or as much as several hundred dollars for interviewing you and your partners, studying the information in your files, visiting your projects, and actually writing descriptions of you, your projects, and the way your firm tackles an assignment.

After you've hired a writer, provide a list of the topics you want to see covered; point out those that are to be emphasized. Explain the general style you prefer; do you want the text to be fast-paced and casual or more serious? Do you like contractions like "we'll" and "here's" or the more formal "we will" and "here is"? Do you want the text written in the first person, with you and your partners referred to as "I" and "we"? Or do you prefer the third person and being called by name or title? Encourage the writer to suggest changes after he or she sees your artwork and talks to the graphic designer; you'll want the text to be compatible with the design. Once the copy is written, do not edit it yourself. If the text is too long for the space available, tell the writer which details you want to retain for the final draft and which information can be deleted.

HAVING THE BROCHURE PRINTED

Your graphic designer and your business associates can suggest printers to consider and those to avoid. Before you have any work done, talk to at least two printers. Study samples of their work for the quality of the color reproduction and the clarity of pictures. Are the folds sharp? Do the samples have "hickeys," spots caused by dust? Did an uneven application of ink cause roller streaks? Is the type broken?

Most printers will quote approximate prices if you tell them how many pages your brochure has, how many colors you'll use, and how many copies you'll need. Give the printer a sample of the paper you would like to use and mention any specialty work that you will need. If the printer will be setting the type, give him or her an approximate word count. Some printers set their own type; others have the job done by professional typesetters. For a more accurate estimate, furnish the printer with a copy of your text and a photocopy of your mechanical or the dummy brochure that your designer has made up. Specify the size and number of pages, typefaces, number of halftones, number of copies, due date, and other details in writing. Remember to mention if you'll include a credit line for the printer. How much time a printer needs to produce an estimate depends on his or her work load, but you'll usually have the figure within a couple of days.

INSTEAD OF A BROCHURE...

For many reasons you may not need or want a printed and bound brochure. You may be starting a business and have little to show and even less money for printing; you may not have the time to assemble pictures, text, and artwork for the printer; or you may want a presentation that looks professional but is clearly tailored to one specific client. Here are some suggestions on displaying your work in "brochure-like" presentations.

Presentation Albums

You can display photographs, renderings, and plans of one or more projects in the binders with transparent sleeves that are used for architectural awards program entries. The FUL-VU

CB-10 album manufactured by Cooks, Inc. and the twenty-four-pocket Rexel Nyrex Slim-View display book are two examples; at an art or office supply store, you'll find them and similar binders. If you use a three-ring or multi-ring binder like the Kingsbacher Murphy books, you can add as many pages as you need.

Here are the materials that you might include in a presentation on one design project:

Title page: the name of the project and the firm's name printed in dry transfer letters on white or pale opaque paper.

Second page (reverse of title page): two or three paragraphs of information about the project typed with a dark ribbon and a headline of dry transfer letters.

Third page (facing second page): a photograph of the project.

Fourth page: a photostat of the site plan.

Fifth page: a close-up photograph of the project.

Sixth page: a photostat of the floor plan.

Seventh page: an interior view of the project.

Eighth page: the names of the people from your firm who worked on this project and a list of the consultants.

Ninth page: a reprint of a magazine feature on the project.

Tenth page (faces inside of back cover): an aerial photograph of the project.

This presentation is easy to prepare and it can be quickly changed. When you no longer need it, the binder can be used for another presentation or an awards program entry. The pictures can go into the file or off to a magazine or newspaper editor. And this brochure is economical: it should cost you no more than $100, including the binder, the professional enlargements of photographs, the photostats, and the dry transfer lettering. To reduce the cost, use photocopies of plans instead of photostats. Substitute pictures that you've taken yourself or the photographer's proofs for enlargements. To display 4 × 5-inch proofs attractively, mat them with lightweight cardboard that's cut to conceal their edges.

Scrapbooks

Plans, renderings, sales literature, clippings, reprints, and other material from projects can be mounted in scrapbooks. To display pictures, use the self-stick photograph album pages with adhesive surfaces and protective transparent covers. These photo albums range in price from $2 to $25. Additional pages and extension posts are available for more expensive albums.

Folders

If you like the idea of unbound materials that can be combined in many different ways, substitute photocopies of typewritten data sheets for printed material and inexpensive pocket portfolios for the custom-made folders. Sold at office supply houses, the portfolios cost about forty cents each. Firms like Duo-Tang Manufacturing Products Company also make pocket portfolios with brads for attaching sheets that have been drilled on a three-hole punch.

If you'll need several hundred portfolios or folders, ask your printer if he or she can cut, fold, and glue glossy cover stock into presentation folders like Figure 11-1 that will display your material. Or, for a single folder, buy lightweight cardboard at the art store and cut and fold it into shape yourself.

"SETTING" TYPE WITHOUT A PRINTER

To set type without a printer, use hand lettering, stencils and templates, adhesive-backed letters, rubber stamps, and your typewriter. Dry transfer letters that reproduce well can be rubbed onto paper or acrylic sheets. You can buy sheets of the letters in several typefaces and colors at office supply and

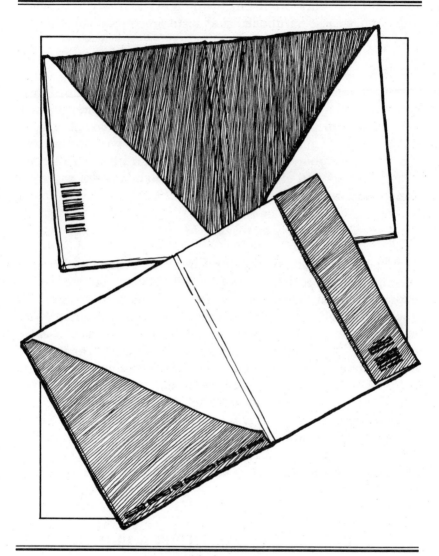

FIGURE 11-1   FOLDERS

If you order large quantities a printer may charge as little as one cent each to make presentation folders like these for you.

art stores. Look for brands like Chartpak, Letraset, Prestype, and Zipatone. For artwork and borders, use rubber stamps, stencils, inked lines, and dry transfers. Graphic art and drafting tapes can be used to create charts, graphs, and designs. These tapes are made in straight and wavy lines in different widths and in holiday, floral, leaf, star, and box patterns. You can buy matching corners to complete borders. Drawings of trees, people, and furniture, and patterns like waves, brick, and pebbles are examples of the artwork available on pressure-sensitive sheets. Besides the standard art and letters, you can buy custom dry transfers. Some of the dry transfer manufacturers will make up tapes and sheets with your name or logo for as little as $50. For more information, check the custom section of the dry transfer catalogs that are available in many art stores.

To add color to individual presentations, use dry transfer typewriter accent symbols and the adhesive-backed dots made in sizes from $\frac{1}{4}$ inch to $1\frac{1}{4}$ inch diameter by Avery Label and Dennison. At an office supply store you'll also find packing seals, foil stars in several sizes and colors, and red and gold legal and notarial seals. Don't overlook the gift wrapping seals made by companies like Hallmark; you can buy foil heart and fruit seals that are appropriate for some presentations.

ANNOUNCEMENTS, HOLIDAY GREETINGS, AND NEWSLETTERS

Keeping editors and your clients informed about your firm's projects, products, and staff members is the obvious reason for sending out announcements, holiday greetings, newsletters, and other office publications. These are valuable for two other important reasons: they boost the morale of your employees by providing recognition, and they keep clients and potential clients aware of your firm's accomplishments. Because all of these mailing pieces may be seen by the same people, they should be designed and written to work together as well as alone. Make sure they're compatible with your stationery, business cards, and brochure.

Content and Design

When you're telling people that you've changed your address or your firm name or that you've added a partner or a product line, when you're thanking them for their patronage during the past year or inviting them to join you for wine and cheese, use a postcard or a poster, a single card or a folder. Use a photograph, a cartoon, or a parody of a formal engraved announcement. Whatever the design, make sure that you've included all the important information. If you're announcing a new address, include the effective date and mention whether you're retaining the same telephone number. If you're announcing a staff promotion, ask the employee if he or she wants his or her full name or a nickname used; include both the person's new and former positions. When you invite people to an office reception, send them the date, the time, and directions.

For an example of an announcement that was designed to be both inexpensive and a caricature of the firm, see Figure 11-2. Used by Wudtke Watson Davis, Inc. and its subsidiary WME to announce a change of address, the card was printed on one side and trimmed to postcard size to cut printing costs, to eliminate the need for envelopes, and to reduce postage costs from fifteen to ten cents a card. The cards were addressed by hand by the children of the firm's partners during a summer vacation. Eric Engstrom, WME president, provided the artwork, a cartoon of principal Don Wudtke at the wheel of his overloaded van. The firms' names were typeset so that they could easily be removed from the mechanical and used with other printing jobs.

If you have several news "stories" to report, save time and money by presenting all of the information in one publication. This allows you to tell your clients what is happening at your firm without sending them different announcements every week for several months. For example, if you've recently moved your office, hired and promoted

We're Moving!
After July 7, 1980
Our Offices will be
located at
200 Green Street
San Francisco 94111

Wudtke Watson Davis, Inc.
Planning/Architecture/Design
(415) 398-0200

WME
Interior Architecture/Space Planning/Design
(415) 398-0213

Please note that our offices will be
closed on July 3, 1980.

FIGURE 11–2   CHANGE OF ADDRESS ANNOUNCEMENT

several employees, and introduced a new product, your news-letter might include a short story on your new address and telephone number. In a longer article you can describe the new offices, mentioning how much more floor space and parking you now have. Other stories will list the people whom you've hired and promoted, with a paragraph or two on each person's training, experience, and new position. The final story can describe the new product line: how it complements your existing lines, how it will be sold, and how you will promote it.

This newsletter may be a one-time publication; you can headline it "We've had a very good year . . ." and use it for your holiday greeting. Or it can be the first of regular monthly, quarterly, or semi-annual issues. If the newsletter is to be a continuing publication, select a design that will accommodate all of the photographs, pictures, and artwork that you may someday want to include. It may be a mock newspaper with three narrow columns of type and mug shots or a folder with large pictures and short stories. Or it may be a chatty one-page letter signed by you. Whether you design the newsletter yourself with a typewriter and dry transfer lettering or turn it over to a graphic designer and printer, remember the newsletter should be easy to read. Use large type, no more than two type styles, and generous margins and gutters.

In a newsletter that's sent to clients and editors, avoid bowling scores, birth announcements, and personal notes that belong only in internal publications. Be consistent in your writing style; if you refer to one employee by his or her first name, refer to all employees that way. If you abbreviate a state's name in one story, don't spell it out in the next. Use short sentences and vary your sentence structure; if the first two sentences in a paragraph are "subject-predicate" in construction, start the third sentence with a descriptive phrase. For example:

John Jones is the new western region sales manager. He replaces Ted Brown, who retired last month. Formerly the central region assistant sales manager, Jones joined us in 1980.

not:

John Jones is the new western region sales manager. He replaces Ted Brown, who retired last month. Jones was formerly the central region assistant sales manager. He joined us in 1980.

Scheduling

How much time you'll need to produce an announcement, an invitation, or a newsletter depends on how much information you must gather before you can start to write, how fast you write, whether pictures must be taken, the complexity of the printing job, and your printer's workload. Allow extra time for your other responsibilities and for the inevitable interruptions. Remember addressing and mailing your publication will take at least a couple of hours. Allow more time if you will have to make up a mailing list.

MAILING LISTS

When you put together your first mailing list, ask everyone on your staff for the names of people who should be included. List your former and current clients, your consultants, public relations people, and the reporters and editors for local, regional, and national publications. Don't forget the people you've made presentations to, even if you haven't received the jobs. If you have sales representatives, ask them for the names of customers they can't see regularly. Add your sales representatives, your distributors, and your dealers. The most important people on your list are your prospective clients and the people who can introduce you to—or recommend you to—prospective clients.

How do you meet prospective clients? Many of them you already know; they're those former classmates, students, and employees who now work for corporations or government agencies that could use your products and services. Who can introduce you to prospective clients? Your banker, your attorney, your suppliers, your real estate broker, your consultants, trade journal editors, the people you've met at Chamber of Commerce and alumni association meetings—and perhaps even your neighbors, your friends, and the parents of your children's friends.

Once you've made a list and edited it, you'll need a method of filing the names and addresses. Some firms list their contacts on index cards that are color-coded by group: clients, consultants, and friends. Other firms use color-coded cards in rotary card files. Still others type the names on master lists that are stored in a three-ring binder or a file drawer; when a mailing is planned, the names are copied onto adhesive labels with a photocopy machine.

Cross file the names on your list by geographic location. Whenever you're planning a trip, consult the list for the names of prospective clients and editors you would like to see. Jot down the date of your visit and the names of the people you met on the lower portion of the index cards.

By keeping your list accurate, you'll ensure that announcements and newsletters get to people on time and you'll avoid having mail returned because of incorrect addresses. Revise your list regularly—before every mailing, every quarter, or, in very small firms, once a year. To save time, do all the revisions at one time. To collect address changes and the names of people who should be added to the list, keep a 5 × 7-inch or larger envelope on the desk where you sort your mail. When you receive notices of address and firm name changes, drop them in this envelope. When you return from a meeting or a presentation, add the business cards of people who should receive your mailing.

DIRECT MAIL

Direct mail is advertising sent through the mail. It may be addressed to a person, to a firm, or simply to "occupant." Most of us call it "junk mail." It may be a letter—a form letter that begins "Dear Friend" or a computer-customized note that opens with the recipient's name. It may be a folder, a postcard, a broadside, a booklet, or a brochure. It may be a self-mailer or may be inserted in an envelope. Whatever its format, a direct mail piece must be designed with the recipient in mind; you must make the recipient curious enough to open it and start reading your message.

What you have to say will help determine which format you select. Try a short message on a postcard as a reminder. When you have more information to convey, send a folder—a single piece of paper printed on both sides and folded once or twice. Or use a broadside, a large (often poster-size) piece that is read as it is unfolded. For a lengthy message and for catalogs and directories, use a booklet. Send a single piece or a combination of several. Somewhere in your package, include a specific offer and a response device—a toll-free telephone number, a postage-paid postcard or envelope, or a coupon.

How to Mail Your Piece

For the most cost-effective direct mail program, carefully select the people who will receive your flyer or booklet. You need to reach those people who want what you're offering and can afford it. For example, if you are an interior designer who can't afford to travel far from your office in Boston, mail only to those people within a two-hour drive. If you do residential interiors, mail to homes, real estate agents, relocation agencies, and the personnel offices that help company executives who are moving to your area. Direct your mail to people in the upper income brackets who probably can afford your services, not to students and factory workers.

Mailing lists—or, more accurately, sets of labels from mailing lists—are available from many magazine publishers. If you're an interior designer, you might buy the names of subscribers to *Architectural Digest*. If you are a small business management consulting firm, buy the names of subscribers to *Inc*. magazine. Some associations also sell the names and addresses of their members. Some lists are available from local chapters of the organizations; others must be ordered from state or national headquarters. You'll also find companies that specialize in compiling and selling lists. From them you can order the names of people in certain professions, geographic areas, and high-income neighborhoods. To find the names of list-sellers in your area, ask your mailing house or your printer. Check the Yellow Pages under "mailing lists" or *Direct Mail List Rates and Data*, a Standard Rate & Data Service publication available in your library.

Before you buy a list, ask the list-seller's marketing representative how the lists are compiled. Some firms simply copy names and addresses from telephone books. You'll also want to know if the names and addresses are listed in ZIP code order and how often the lists are updated. Another question: Are you buying the names of firms or of individuals? If you order a list of every architect and interior designer in a city rather than a list of the architectural and interior design firms, most firms will receive two, three, or even four copies of the same mailer. This duplication is costly, and it creates a "junk mail" image with the person sorting the mail. However, duplication does increase the probability that your message will reach the people most interested in your products and services.

Compare the available lists carefully. The list of 2,500 firm names that is revised monthly may cost $60 per 1,000 names and $150 for computer time, but it won't have the duplication and inaccurate addresses of a less expensive list of individuals that is updated only once a year. Ask list-sellers to guarantee that only a small percentage of the labels they sell you will have incorrect addresses or the names of defunct firms. Lists are sold in different ways. Some are sold for a flat fee. Others have a minimum charge plus a fee per name. In 1980, some professional associations were charging ten cents per name; some publishers were charging $60 per 1,000.

Often you can buy names and addresses on 3 × 5-inch cards, on adhesive labels not intended for machine application, on magnetic computer tape, or on Cheshire labels that can be applied with a machine. The least expensive list usually is the membership roster from which you'll have to type your own labels.

For about $50 per 1,000 pieces, mailing houses will label your flyers or insert letters in envelopes. They will sort your direct mail pieces by ZIP code and deliver them to the appropriate postal terminal. If you want to mail with a third-class bulk rate permit, you can rent the mailing house's permit for $40 a year. (If you will be renting a permit, select your mailing house and obtain its number before you have your mailing pieces printed. The bulk rate permit number usually is printed on the mailing piece.)

To find a mailing house, ask advertising and public relations people for recommendations. Your printer and graphic designer also may have suggestions. Call several mailing houses and ask for price estimates. When you decide which mailing house you'll be using, ask for the name of the person who will coordinate your mailing. This is especially important if the mailing will include several different pieces that are sent to the mailing house separately. For example, a publisher might be sending reprints of a magazine feature, a printer the cover letter, and a supplier the custom-made envelopes. In a letter to the mailing house, list all the pieces that are to be mailed and the order in which they are to be inserted in the envelope. Mention the approximate date the pieces will arrive at the mailing house and the date by which you'd like the pieces mailed. Before the pieces are mailed, the mailing house will ask you for a check to cover the estimated postage and most of the handling fee. Most houses will invoice you for the remaining ten or fifteen percent of your bill.

Postage

If you mail fewer than 900 direct mail pieces each year, first-class postage may be more economical than third-class bulk rate because of the cost of the bulk rate permit. The annual fee for a bulk rate permit is $40; the fee for an imprint permit, which allows you to print your bulk rate permit number on your mailing piece, is an additional $30. The imprint permit is valid if you use it at least once each year. These fees bring the cost of the first 1,000 pieces that you mail third-class bulk rate yourself to $174—the $70 in permits plus 10.4 cents per one-ounce piece. (Postcards are less.) You'll save the $30 imprint fee if you use a mailing house's permit, but you'll pay a handling fee. If the mailing house charges $50 per 1,000 pieces, your cost would be $194—the $40 for the permit, $104 in postage, and $50 in mailing charges. In contrast, mailing 1,000 pieces first class in 1981 cost only $180. First-class mail does not have to be sorted by ZIP code and it'll receive better service, too; third-class mail can take weeks to be delivered and it is sometimes lost. For nonprofit groups, the third-class bulk rate is substantially less. In 1981, when the regular third-class bulk rate charge per piece was 10.4 cents, the nonprofit charge was 3.5 cents. This means that a nonprofit group's cost of mailing 1,000 pieces would be $105, including all permits, or $125 with a mailing house.

To use a third-class bulk rate permit, your mailing pieces must be identical and sorted by ZIP code. You must mail at least 200 pieces or fifty pounds whenever you use the permit. The postage must be paid several days in advance of the mailing. For more information, call your postmaster or the Bulk Mail Center in your area.

When you use first-class mail, you can use stamps in sheets or rolls of 100 or 500. Your envelopes can also be sent through the postage meter in your office.

12

YOUR OFFICE IS A MARKETING TOOL, TOO

Put this book down and walk out your office door. Stroll down the hall or out to the curb. Close your eyes for a minute and try to forget how well you know this building and the reception area of your office. Now, as you walk back, pretend you're a prospective customer coming to the office for the first time. What do you see? Peeling paint and dirty windows? Spindly furniture that you hesitate to use? Fussy wallpaper and ruffled cushions that suggest a boudoir? Drooping plants and dusty tabletops? A desk covered with papers and littered with coffee cups, soggy french fries, and an overflowing ashtray?

Ask yourself what this office tells your clients about you. What is their first impression? Organized—or haphazard? Discreet—or ostentatious? Good taste—or schlock? Now think about how the reception area makes people feel. Is it a somber, dreary room that depresses them? A stage set that intimidates them with its perfection? Or is it a warm, inviting place where people are comfortable waiting?

Your office can help you market yourself. How? That's what this chapter is all about. Intended for anyone who brings customers and editors into an office, this chapter provides lots of suggestions for office displays—and the names of products and processes that you can use to assemble these displays yourself. You'll also find reminders on making your office attractive and easy to find.

BEFORE YOU WALK IN THE DOOR

Take a look at your office building from the street; how easily can a stranger find you? If the building is difficult to see from the street, can you put up a sign that points visitors in the right direction? If you already have a sign, check it from a couple of blocks away in each direction; is the sign easy to see, especially if you're driving? Or is it blocked by a neighbor's sign? Are some of the lights burned out? Is the paint faded? Are the street numbers and the building name clearly visible from the street? How much trouble would a stranger have finding the building after dark or on a winter morning when drifts of snow hide signs?

Now think about where your office visitors park. If you don't have a parking lot, have you rented spaces at a nearby lot or arranged to pay for visitor parking at a garage? Tell your clients about parking facilities and, if possible, post signs that show them where to leave their cars. If your building has its own parking, look at the lot carefully. Is it littered with leaves and papers or does the building manager keep the pavement swept? Does rain water run off or are there puddles everywhere? Are the garbage cans concealed? Are spaces near the building reserved for the handicapped and for visitors?

As you approach the building, is the main entrance obvious? Are there curb cuts and ramps for people in wheelchairs? Are the doors easy to open, even when it's windy and rainy? Look at the landscaping; are the plants healthy? Are the planters choked with weeds? Is the grass cut frequently?

201

If there's a flagpole, look up at the flags. Are they faded and ragged? Is there a spotlight to illuminate the flags after dark or does the building manager come out at sunset to retire them?

NOW THAT YOU'RE INSIDE...

Continue to think of yourself as a stranger as you walk into the building. If it's a large building, is the directory easy to find? Is your name on the directory and spelled correctly? In a smaller building, have you marked the direction to your office? On your door, do you have an attractive sign that's been designed to complement your business cards, stationery, brochure, and office interiors? If you work by yourself or with a small staff and you sometimes are all gone at the same time, post your office hours and indicate if messages and packages can be left with your neighbor or the building manager.

In your office foyer, is there someone to greet your visitors and tell you that they've arrived? If you have no one to relieve your receptionist when he or she takes a lunch break and runs errands, post a neatly lettered sign listing every staff member's extension. Invite your visitors to announce themselves by dialing the appropriate number. Keep the walls in the reception area washed and painted, the carpet and the upholstery clean, the furniture dusted. Stack the magazines, newspapers, and product brochures neatly or arrange them in racks. Make sure that you have a couple of comfortable chairs, a coatrack, and an umbrella stand. Today, many offices have signs that ask their visitors not to smoke; in other offices, ashtrays are hidden to discourage smoking. If you don't mind if your clients smoke, keep ashtrays in clear view. Clean them frequently.

SHOW OFF YOUR WORK

Make it easy for your visitors to learn something about you and your work before you even introduce yourself or make a presentation. Leave an office brochure or copies of your product catalogs in the reception room; decorate foyers, hallways, and conference rooms with reprints and clippings of stories about you and your projects, whether pictures of your projects and products have been splashed across the cover of *The New York Times* or nearly hidden in the back pages of a small town newspaper. Use photographs, drawings, samples, models, award certificates, and exhibits that show how your products are manufactured and used. Or display an eye-catching collection—a dozen antique toy cars, old orange crate labels, or a wooden carousel steed—that will both interest your visitors and help you get a friendly conversation started. To display the reprints, photocopies of clippings, and catalogs that your visitors can take with them, use wire literature racks, display boxes you build yourself from cardboard, or the wall-mounted high tech plastic storage units that are sold in different sizes in housewares stores.

If you pin reprints up on bulletin boards, you can change the displays whenever you have new clippings to add. In your conference room, you can combine the reprints with drawings and photographs of projects that will interest a potential client. Use cork, painted or left natural, or a soft panel that can be painted to match or contrast with the walls. You can put a bulletin board by the entry or run an eighteen-inch-wide strip of molding-trimmed cork around the room. You can panel a door, part of a wall—or all the walls—with the soft wood.

To keep reprints and clippings clean and to prevent them from curling and tearing, frame these copies of stories with standard frames that you assemble yourself. Protect clippings of nearly any size in the simple plastic box frames made by firms like Dax and sold in many housewares stores. Or you can slip the reprints between sheets of glass or acrylic that are fastened together with the clips found in art supply and frame shops. These frames come apart easily so that you can quickly change the displays. For more permanent exhibits, use the metal frame kits that you can assemble yourself. Brands like Framekit are sold two lengths to a package, so that you can build frames in unusual sizes like 5 × 14 inches or 10 × 20 inches as well as the standard 5 × 7, 8 × 10, 11 × 14, and 16 × 20-inch sizes.

Dry mount copies of your features, too. Use a can of dry mount spray or sheets of dry mount adhesive, stiff cardboard from an art store, and a squeegee. You can have reprints professionally mounted by one of the firms listed under "photographic mounts" in the Yellow Pages. For more dramatic displays, have photographs and articles like reviews and cover stories copied, enlarged, and mounted.

You can frame or mat black-and-white and color prints of any size; for an idea of what oversize prints cost, ask your lab or a custom printer for price estimates on $8\frac{1}{2}$ × 11 and 11 × 14-inch enlargements. You can frame or mount larger pictures and use them in groups, as posters, or as murals. Have black-and-white pictures printed in black and white, or ask your photographer to use a sepia bleach and toner. Have high-contrast or textured prints made of black-and-white or color photographs; ask your photographer, a printer, or a photography lab for samples and cost estimates. If your foyer is dark or you would like to hang a picture of your work in a dimly lit hallway, have a transparency copied, enlarged, and backlit. There are two ways to have this done. You can ask a reliable color lab or your photographer to copy your slide or 4 × 5-inch transparency. If Cibacrome film is used, the duplicate is less likely to fade. Or ask the lab for high-contrast prints. Have a silk screen printer make separations; you'll need four if you have a full color transparency. Then have the images screened onto a clear or frosted acetate film. Have an exhibit house construct an illuminated box and slip your picture between two sheets of glass at the front. Use a small, cool light in the box to keep the transparency from overheating or fading.

Before you have reprints or photographs to display, show off your drawings. Order extra blueprints of your designs or of designs that have been done for you (like your office building). Use marking pens to add some color, and then have the prints mounted and shrink-wrapped at a frame shop or a mounting house. Hang models and samples on the wall or display them on shelves, on tabletops, or in a cabinet that looks like an old-fashioned store's bay window. Suspend your samples from the ceiling with fishing line or hang them on the walls with cup hooks.

Display your awards certificates where clients will have time to study them; if you hang the certificates in your reception area, office visitors can glance at the awards while they're waiting for you. Make sure that the certificates are neatly framed with identical or complementary materials. Think about matting the most important certificates in a color that contrasts with the frames and your walls. Hang up copies of the awards certificates received by the people you've commissioned, too; ask for duplicate certificates when a graphic artist is cited for the design of your annual report, and when an advertising agency is recognized for the advertisements that it wrote for your products. If you cannot obtain duplicate certificates, borrow the originals and have photostats made.

Show off examples of what other firms have done for you, too; hang up the slicks from your new advertising campaign, the sketches of the uniforms that are being made for your employees, and an oversized copy of the new label that you've had designed.

Frame your professional licenses, your diplomas, and the certificates from continuing education programs. Hang them on the wall behind your desk or in a hallway with the certificates earned by other members of your firm.

Assemble exhibits that explain how your product is made or how your office delivers a service. If you make furniture, show where you obtain your raw materials with striking photographs that have been made into high-contrast prints, enlarged, and mounted. Show the drops of dew on trees at sunrise, the sheep grazing in the field, the flax in bloom, and the cotton being harvested. Then add a sample of the wood you use, a cotton boll, the flax yarn, and the carded wool. Dry mount and hang a blueprint of a chair and a photograph of the looms. If you run an advertising agency, show each step of a commercial that you've made: the script, the storyboard,

FIGURE 12-1   OFFICE INTERIOR
Old tools and office equipment are displayed in the reception area of the John F. Otto Service Center, a California construction firm headquartered in Sacramento's historic district.

FIGURE 12–2   CONFERENCE ROOM PREPARED FOR A MEETING
Partners at Backen, Arrigoni & Ross, Inc., a San Francisco architectural firm, prepare for presentations by posting drawings and photographs of the firm's work on the conference room bulletin boards.

the actors and director on the set, and a still photograph from the finished commercial.

Or put together an exhibit that shows how your product and its uses have changed through the years. If you sell restaurant equipment, combine photographs of turn-of-the century restaurant kitchens with copies of early sales orders and your first product brochures. Add pictures of your first models in use; follow these with pictures of the most significant improvements in the equipment and a chart that compares the cost, capacity, and energy consumption of your first and current models.

Use your displays to emphasize your key marketing points. If you run a locally operated dairy that promotes itself as a family farm, use copies of pictures from your family album on the walls of your retail outlets. To emphasize your firm's continuing research and development, make your exhibit a bold time line, with samples or pictures of every new model and product improvement.

13

SPEECHES AND SLIDE PRESENTATIONS

Speaking, like writing a press release, is a valuable public relations skill. With a speech, you can say something about yourself and your business to at least three different groups: the people who attend the speech, the people who hear quotes from it, and the people who read newspaper reports of it. Speaking, like being published, gives you credibility; when you stand behind the podium, you'll be regarded as an expert.

With slide presentations you can both say and show something about yourself and your business. Your program may be a general survey of your work or a carefully planned presentation for an important client; you may use slides to illustrate a speech at the Chamber of Commerce or for a presentation at the high school Career Day.

There's nothing very difficult about a speech or a slide program. Neither one has to be a Hollywood production; all your audience expects is a logical, accurate presentation on a topic that is important to you and to the people you're speaking to. How you select a topic, how you organize your comments, how you prepare artwork, and, most importantly, how you find an audience are all covered in this chapter.

SPEECHES

Start planning for your speechmaking with a list. Jot down all of the topics that you are prepared to discuss and all the slide presentations and films that you can borrow. Your speech topics might include a history of your firm and industry or a current controversy's effect on prices and supplies. Or you can offer advice on buying your products and services. Put together a speech entitled "How to buy fine jewelry," "Five decisions to make before hiring an advertising agency," or "How to select a printer."

Tell your audience how to do something. If you're a graphic designer, explain how people can design and produce their own Christmas cards; if you're a developer, show them how warehouses can be converted to income-producing office buildings. If you're an accountant, describe how people should handle questions from the Internal Revenue Service. And tell people how others in the same profession are tackling problems that they all share; talk about the marketing programs that other lawyers have started or the help that small businesses are getting from MBA students at nearby campuses.

To illustrate your points, use slides, films, and filmstrips. Don't forget posters, maps, graphs, samples, and models. Display artwork and graphics on flip charts and on transparencies for overhead projectors, too. To help people understand complex or abstract ideas, use familiar objects; if you're explaining how a lathe peels veneer off a log, unwind a roll of paper towels.

Slide shows, films, posters, and the other visual aids that you can use in your presentation are available from many manufacturers, special interest groups, and trade and professional associations. These groups also sell or give away folders and brochures that you can hand out to your audience. To obtain the lists of materials available, write the groups to which you belong and the manufacturers whose products you use. Watch newspapers and magazine articles and advertisements for offers of reprints. Some magazines regularly publish lists of free and inexpensive materials available from companies and trade groups. Ask local museums and public and college libraries about slide programs and films, too.

You can make your own handouts with a few paragraphs of typed text, a headline of dry transfer lettering, and a handdrawn chart or graph. Have these reproduced at your quick copy shop for a few dollars. If you plan to present the same talk several times, work with a graphic designer and a printer for a more professional publication. For suggestions on working with a designer and a printer, see Chapter 11.

Finding an Audience

To give a speech, of course, you must have an audience. Try starting with the groups to which you already belong; if you attend their meetings regularly, you know which topics are most appropriate and which program formats are most popular. Because you know your listeners, you can tailor a general outline to their specific concerns.

If a club's program chairperson has never invited you to speak, don't hesitate to mention your interest. Finding stimulating speakers for every meeting is usually a burden for the people who run club programs; most of them welcome volunteers. All you will probably have to say is something casual like "Great panel you put together for last week's meeting, Joe; really thought-provoking. If you'd ever like to have a program on the new continuing education requirements for doctors, just let me know."

When you are not involved in a group, you may prefer to send a note to the president or program chairperson:

Although I haven't been active in the Chamber, I'd appreciate an opportunity to get to know you and the other members. If you'd like a program for an upcoming meeting, I'll be glad to discuss how the new continuing education requirements for doctors are affecting the cost of everyone's medical care.

When you are invited to address a group, ask the program chairperson how long a presentation you should prepare. If you're considering showing slides or a film, ask if a screen and projector are available and if the room can be darkened.

Outlining Your Speech

Begin your speech with a short introduction. Just as a headline tells a reader what a newspaper story will cover, your introduction will prepare your audience for what you'll say. A quick summary of your most important points will figuratively chart the course for your audience.

To organize your speech, use an inverted pyramid or a historical outline. With the inverted pyramid, begin with the most important information and end with what's least important. With the historical (sometimes called narrative or story line) method, start at the beginning of the story. Let's look at how the same speech would start with these two different outlines. If you used the inverted pyramid to organize your discussion of continuing education requirements, you might open with an estimate of the time and money doctors invest in classes. You would emphasize how these required classes have increased the cost of medical care. With a historical outline, you might begin with a description of the early continuing education programs and then go on to explain why states made the programs mandatory. You would end with estimates of what continuing education now costs doctors and their patients and with comments on pending changes in continuing education legislation.

Whichever method you use to organize the speech, outlining your comments is as simple as making a list. Just note all the points you would like to make. These will probably be such generalizations as "classes are expensive" and "require-ment raises cost of medical care." Number the generaliza-tions in the order in which you'll present them; add statistics, case histories, and examples to explain and substantiate the general statements.

Type your speech or the outline you'll speak from with the largest size type available. Double or triple space and allow a three-inch-wide margin on the right side. If you expect to revise the speech several times, type each paragraph on a separate sheet of paper so that you can add, delete, and reorganize material without retyping the speech.

Read your speech carefully and ask someone else to review it. Is your information correct? Are your sentences short and easy to understand? Have you avoided clichés and offensive terms? Have you explained the statistics and the technical words that you've used? Are your transitions smooth and logical? Have you stayed within the time limit? (For a ten-minute presentation, you will need 1,200 to 2,000 words or five to eight double-spaced pages.)

Use the wide margin of your script for the phonetic spell-ings of words and names that are hard to pronounce. Write notes to remind yourself when to pause, when to gesture, and when to refer to samples, slides, and charts. If you don't have visual aids, use the margin to sketch what you'll have made. Make sure every slide, chart, and graph that you've planned is necessary. Does each one make an important point, or are you using them only because they're all you have?

Practice your speech in front of a mirror or a couple of friends; use a tape recorder if you have one. Try for three rehearsals: a "stagger through," a walk through, and a dress rehearsal with the equipment and artwork that you'll use. Ask your "critics" if you're speaking slowly and loudly enough. Do you sound natural? Are you looking up from your script for eye contact with people in the audience? Think about where you'll put your hands. Try resting them in your pockets or on the edge of the podium. Use one to hold a pointer or the remote control for the slide projector.

The Day of the Speech

If you're new in the community or a stranger to most of those
in the audience, bring a one- or two-paragraph biography that
the program chairperson can use when he or she introduces
you. In this sketch, emphasize what you have in common
with the people to whom you're speaking. For example, if
you're speaking to the Chamber of Commerce in a small community, point out that you're well aware of the problems of
small towns because you've lived and worked in them most of
your life:

> New to Davenport, but not new to the problems of small
> towns. He was reared in a small Kansas town and is a graduate
> of Iowa State University at Ames. His first job was in Auburn,
> California and his second was in Chehalis, Washington.

And point out why you're qualified to speak. If you're a
developer discussing warehouse renovations, list the buildings that you've renovated and leased. If you're an accountant talking about the IRS, tell the program chairperson that
you have worked for the Internal Revenue Service and the
tax auditing departments of two major accounting firms.

If you are speaking to a large group whose meetings attract extensive press coverage, take along a few copies of
your speech for the reporters.

Try to arrive at the meeting early. Check the microphone
and the projector. Set up the charts, graphs, or maps that
you'll use. Once you've done this, relax. Encourage the program chairperson to introduce you to people whom you
haven't met. After your speech, ask for questions. If there's
one you can't answer, take the person's name and address.
Within the next day or so, respond to the question; if you
can't find an answer, at least write the person a short note explaining that you're unable to obtain the information. And
write the program chairperson a note of thanks, too. You
might say:

Once again, I'd like to thank you for the opportunity to speak at yesterday's Chamber meeting. I appreciated meeting so many Chamber members, and I certainly enjoyed our lively discussion on the IRS.

SLIDE PRESENTATIONS

Will your slide program be a presentation in itself? Or will it be a series of illustrations for the key points of your speech? Are you showing the program to one client or the one hundred members of the Garden Club? However you use slides, they should be attractive and easy to see. Your program should be well-organized and short, perhaps only ten minutes. Each slide should make a single point.

Organization

Organize your slide presentations by topics. If you're an architect, assemble a program on a project or on a general building type like single-family residences. Put together a show that illustrates the underground houses that you've designed and a program that shows all of your energy-conserving buildings. If you're a graphic designer, use one presentation to show the business cards and stationery that you've designed and another presentation to show advertisements and package designs for a particular company. When you plan a slide program, remember who will be watching it and what you want to tell them; put together different programs for your clients, your colleagues, and your students.

To organize slides into a program, use a viewing screen, a light table, or a storyboard. A storyboard, a sheet of paper with several small boxes, allows you to plan an entire program in as much detail as you need. You can sketch in the slides you need to have made and write the comments you'll make when each slide is shown. To make your own storyboard, rule off a sheet with 2 × 2-inch or larger frames.

Allow space between each line of frames for captions. If you'll be using two projectors for the slide program, lay out the storyboard with pairs of frames. Slide this guide under the sheet of tracing paper on which you'll work.

To organize slide programs on a variety of topics, you only need a few copies of the same slides. Keep the two or three standard programs you use frequently in slide trays. The other presentations, the one-time programs, can be organized and the number of each slide recorded; then, after they're used, the slides can be returned to the files. When you want a presentation, use a record like Figure 13-1 to reorganize the slides.

If you store all of your slides in the same file, have duplicate slides made for slide programs or mark the slides you use in shows "Slide Program Only: Do Not Remove" so that you won't inadvertently send magazine editors the slides you need.

Slide programs usually include 35mm color photographs and title slides. You can create special effects with synchronized twin projectors and with the two-inch-square "super slides." Add variety with copies of black-and-white photographs, maps, renderings, plans, cartoons, charts, graphs, and text. Besides the familiar pie and bar graphs, you can use a table or matrix, a line graph, an activity and time chart, an organization chart, or a process flow. Select your material carefully to make sure that your slide program won't look like a collection of unrelated pictures.

Because photographs lose some of their clarity when projected, use only clear, sharp pictures and drawings. Redraw maps and plans to eliminate confusing details. Have text and artwork printed in dark colors on light backgrounds for the best contrast. Remember to select type that will be legible from a distance. When projected, your letters should have at least one inch of height for every thirty-two feet of the audience's distance from the screen. If the last row of seats in your meeting room is sixty feet from the screen, your letters should be almost two inches high on the screen.

Most commercial photographers and labs will copy

PRESENTATION FOR: St. Andrew Country Day School, Jackson, Miss.

Date Signed Out: March 6, 1980

Date Returned: March 6, 1980

JOB:	SLIDE NUMBERS:
Huygens and Tappé	Title
Back Bay, Boston	A4, A10
Rivers Country Day #6503	A7, A1, A4, Interior Classroom, Exterior
Longy School	A7, B1, B11, B12
Huygens House #6629	A12, A16, A14
Gerstein House	A16, B5
Awards #6904	A11
Bailey House #6631	B5
Prov. Country Day #6807	A10, B12, B8, C4, C9, C8
Tilton School #7401	Site Plan
Franklin Park Zoo #7321	B2, C18
Loon Mountain #6523	E11
Huygens Chalet #6809	A16
Les Courcelles #7301	Exterior Photo
Pevero Hotel	B1, 29
Lyford Cay Condos #7528	Rendering
Sharjah Aquarium	A8, A24
Concord Greene #7008	Exterior Photo
John Curtis Library #7228	A15, B11
Milford Library	C6, B17
Library Promo #6930	B1
New Hampshire Coll.	A22, B3, New Site, Income Chart, System Selection, B6, B5, B8, A19, B12, Construction Shot, B2, B11, B10, A10, C5, Fieldhouse, Collectors, Athletic Center Interior Stairs, Pool

FIGURE 13-1 SLIDE PROGRAM RECORD

FIGURE **13–1** CONT.

#6631	
Prov. Country Day School	A10
#6930	
New Hampshire Coll.	A19
#6818	
Hazard House	B8
Lyford Cay Condos	Rendering
#6503	
Longy School	B1
#6629	
Gerstein House	B5
#6708	
Vose House	A13
Library Promotion	B1
Rivers Country Day	A6

renderings, maps, and artwork with slide film. You can do the work yourself, too. If you have your own darkroom, mount your camera on the enlarger stand and fasten the artwork to the easel. If you don't have a darkroom, fasten the artwork to a wall that's evenly lit. Focus the camera carefully, filling your viewfinder with the image you're photographing. For the sharpest picture, mount the camera on a tripod and use the smallest aperture opening on the camera. Make several exposures.

You can make title slides in the same way. Use dry transfer letters or hand lettering to print your program title or text on stiff cardboard. You can use dry transfer letters for professional-looking type on plans, maps, and sketches, too. Apply the letters directly to the artwork or to a transparent acrylic sheet that you pin or tape over the artwork before photographing it.

When you need title slides, don't overlook existing signs on buildings, businesses, and highways. Photographed carefully, these may provide exactly the titles you need. In a camera shop, you can buy title slide kits with adhesive-backed letters. You can attach these letters to cardboard or, for more variety in your title slides, to weathered boards, bottles, beach balls, and other uneven surfaces.

Make your title slides fit the topics of your programs: for a presentation on ski resorts, stamp letters in the snow and photograph them. For a program on beachside condominiums, scrawl your titles in the sand or write them on banners that you attach to turrets of a sand castle. If the subject is schools, chalk your text on a blackboard or print it on the oversized ruled paper first graders use. If you're discussing the state fair or an amusement park, paint your titles on balloons.

14

COMMUNITY ACTIVITIES AND TEACHING

One of the best ways to meet people in your community is by participating in local activities. Whether you speak at the Chamber of Commerce meeting or provide seedlings for the Arbor Day observance, show high school students your factory or judge 4-H livestock at the county fair, you'll meet potential clients. You're also likely to meet the press. Reporters attend civic club meetings and photographers turn up at tree-planting ceremonies; school district publicists join tours and television crews seldom miss the color and excitement of a local fair competition.

Teaching—at a neighborhood adult education center or a prestigious Ivy League college—is another way of meeting potential clients. The people who take your classes will always regard you as an expert in your field. Many of them will turn to you when they need advice. Teaching will also enhance your credentials and give you speaking experience. And you'll probably make a little money and meet people who are interested in working for you.

This chapter suggests contributions that you can make in your community. It also addresses the question of how you can benefit from community activities. Later, you'll find suggestions for starting a part-time teaching career and a discussion of teaching's potential rewards.

COMMUNITY ACTIVITIES

Before you decide which groups to join and which projects to tackle, consider how much time and money you have to offer and what you can gain from each activity. Where will you meet the most potential clients? Which activities offer the most media coverage? And, most importantly, what will give you the greatest personal satisfaction? Make most of your activities business-related; your expenses may be tax-deductible and you'll be able to demonstrate the quality of your work. You'll also have the opportunity to explain your services and their importance.

If you're a florist, judge floral arrangements at the Rose Show. Demonstrate how to make corsages to Garden Club members or organize a "Christmas around the world" display of trees and wreaths for a local bank. If you run a hardware store, tell the Homemakers' Club about the newest house paints and inexpensive disposable brushes. Or show the Boy Scouts how to replace the plug on an electric can opener. If you manufacture furniture, offer the Lions Club a tour of your factory or reupholster an antique divan for the historical museum.

You can write a column for the local paper, too; if you sell cookware, write a weekly feature on recipes. If you run a nursery, put together several stories for the spring gardening edition. If you're a contractor, tell the editor that you will write a regular question-and-answer column on building and remodeling. Or help the Visitors' Bureau with its projects; provide the pictures for a brochure on architectural landmarks, design the map for a sightseeing guide to the city, or print the posters for a community art festival.

Use your hobbies to meet people who can help you, too. Suppose you're a veterinarian who plays the commodity markets; why not organize a panel discussion for the Businessmen's Alliance on investing? If you're a custom home builder who sails, show slides of your most recent cruise at the yacht club meeting. If you're an accountant with a flair for Chinese cooking, donate a dinner for twelve cooked by yourself to the public television station's fund-raising auction.

Don't overlook the traditional activities. Join the theater group, the symphony supporters, or the Friends of the Library. Participate in your church, your block association, or your alumni group. Organize a Sunday tour of homes to benefit a local charity. Serve on a school planning or neighborhood improvement committee. Run for city council, school board, or the hospital commission.

How will these activities benefit you? If you judge at the Rose Show, you'll meet other judges and show officials and you may have your name printed in agate-size type in the show program. When you decorate Christmas trees for the bank lobby, you'll meet the banker—a valuable contact and a potential customer. Every bank customer will see your artistry—and your name on the "Compliments of . . ." placard displayed near the trees. You'll probably find your special holiday exhibit pictured in the local paper, too.

If you're the accountant who donates catering services to a fund-raising auction, you'll be mentioned—perhaps even featured—in the newspaper stories about contributions to the auction. You'll meet the auction's socialite organizers and the dinner guests, all potential clients. If you join a block association or serve on a school planning committee, your neighbors or fellow committee members are likely to be reporters, bankers, lawyers, government officials, and other small business people. Some may become clients; others will recommend you to their friends and associates. Still others will help you with your first press release, your application for a Small Business Administration loan, or your plans for an addition to your building.

Whether you're working with the Cub Scouts or the Kiwanis, the symphony or the school board, keep the press informed. Send editors advance and follow-up stories on your activities; write a press release a couple of weeks before you demonstrate how to make corsages or change plugs. Send the paper a brief report on the symphony association's new officers after the election meeting; announce the new hot lunch prices after the school board budget session.

Remember to call the newspapers whenever you expect an event to result in good pictures; let the appropriate editor know when the preschool class is finger painting with chocolate pudding or the first graders are planting fir seedlings. A slender Sunday school teacher struggling to break ground for a new church building or a businessman swathed in a butcher-style apron and chef's hat would also make a good photograph. There are the standard pictures, too: the group photo of the new officers, the historical society president accepting a donation, the table setting that illustrates a feature on summer brunches.

TEACHING

Start your teaching career with guest appearances at your alma mater or at classes taught by your friends. You'll learn whether you like teaching and whether you can stimulate students and give them the information they need. You'll also gain some experience and make contacts that will be helpful if you decide to pursue a regular part-time teaching position.

If you're a mechanic, speak to the high school driver education class; if you run an advertising agency, speak to marketing students. If you're a graphic designer, discuss brochures with architectural students or menus with hotel administration students. If you're a tax attorney, organize a panel of lawyers and accountants to speak to law students.

You can teach at a community college or university, in a graduate school's extension program, or in one of the many adult education centers across the country. Some programs carry course credit; others offer continuing education credit from professional associations or the schools themselves. A third group of programs carry no credit; they're designed for the participants' pleasure and education.

Besides providing excellent exposure for business people, these programs allow you to share your concerns with people who have similar interests. Many program directors welcome ideas and outlines for new classes from professionals who would like to teach. Sometimes these suggestions are too academic or so narrow in focus that the classes would be difficult to fill; other proposals duplicate classes already being offered. With modification, however, many ideas proposed by community members result in classes. Some are taught as one- or two-day seminars, some as week-long workshops, and others for a couple of hours one night a week for several weeks.

Because the supply of teachers usually exceeds the demand and because educational institutions, regardless of their stature, have limited budgets, compensation for part-time teachers is low. Professionals with no teaching experience and those teaching in special programs receive especially low salaries. At the Harvard University Graduate School of Design, beginning teachers in the special program received $300 a teaching day in 1980. Just a few blocks away, at the unaccredited Cambridge Center for Adult Education, teachers received as little as $150 for an entire course. At some degree-granting schools like the Boston Architectural Center, most instructors receive no salary. Other private colleges pay from $15 to $40 an hour. Tax-supported community colleges pay part-time instructors according to a standard salary schedule.

In some schools, suggesting a class requires little more than submitting an outline and meeting with the program directors. In others, you may be hired to teach an existing course with a well-organized teaching plan.

Does teaching help you build a client list? Some people say yes; others say no. Barbara Welanetz, a marketing consultant who taught a course on marketing professional services at the Cambridge Center for Adult Education, said

If you are	You can
managing any business or nonprofit organization	describe the job opportunities in your field to high school or college students with a speech, a panel discussion, or an article in the local or school paper.
a beautician	make up models for a charity fashion; or speak on skin and hair care at girls' club meetings; or write a question-and-answer column for the women's page of the local newspaper.
a carpenter	teach woodworking or home improvement classes through college extension programs; or write a feature story on how to select and maintain tools.
a copywriter	describe typical problems with business writing at the Chamber of Commerce meeting; or teach a course on writing advertising copy at the adult education center.
a lawyer	speak on consumer protection laws at the homemakers' meeting; or organize a legal advice hotline.

If you	You can
operate an inn	donate a weekend's lodging to a fund-raising auction; or conduct a tour of your restaurant kitchen for the gourmet cooking class.
raise Christmas trees	donate trees to the local hospitals; describe the size and importance of the Christmas tree industry in speeches to business groups; or show slides of the different species of trees to a home decorating class.
sell farm implements	describe your equipment to 4-H Club members; help restore antique farm equipment at the historical museum; or chauffeur the fair queen through a local parade on your latest model tractor.

FIGURE 14-1 SAMPLE COMMUNITY ACTIVITIES FOR BUSINESS PEOPLE

227

many of her students had only a casual interest in running their own businesses. And those who were in business for themselves couldn't afford to hire her. In contrast, landscape architect Leah Haygood often finds herself working as a consultant to former students from the University of California at Berkeley. Many of her students take jobs in government and institutions; as they advance into management positions, they need outside help. "A former student working in a park department, with universities, water districts, the U.S. Army Corps of Engineers, or the Forest Service is a veritable gold mine," she pointed out.

15

THERE'S NOTHING VERY COMPLICATED ABOUT MARKETING

There's nothing very complicated about marketing. Like everything else in this book, it requires courtesy, common sense—and the answers to a couple of very simple questions. First, what do your customers really want? Secondly, how can you persuade them that you can meet their needs?

You're probably thinking that this sounds deceptively easy. You're right: the questions are simple, but finding the answers takes some work. That's what this chapter is for. In the pages that follow, you'll find some of the reasons why people buy products and services; you'll learn how to recognize these reasons; and you'll consider many different ways of marketing yourself to both your present and prospective customers.

WHY DO PEOPLE BUY?

Why do people buy? Not because they want what you're selling. You sell things; people only want what those things can do for them. If you run a pharmacy, you sell aspirin and antibiotics; your customers buy relief from pain and infection. If you operate a Ferrari dealership, you sell cars; your customers buy adventure, glamour, and prestige. If you run a fast food franchise, you sell hot dogs, hamburgers, and fishwiches; your customers buy quick service, a familiar menu, and moderate prices. If you're a builder, you sell houses; your customers buy homes. If you design dresses, you sell clothes; your customers buy illusion.

The way you sell is a part of what your customers buy, too. The man who rummages through discount houses and factory outlets buys low price and the satisfaction of a bargain. The woman who uses a mail order catalog buys convenience; she can shop at any hour without getting dressed, hiring a babysitter, driving through traffic, struggling to find a parking place, and trudging from one store to another. If you sell kits, your customers have the opportunity to create. If you accept credit cards, your customers buy financing; if you offer demonstrations, they buy trial runs. If you deliver their orders promptly, they buy reliability.

What else do people buy? The opportunity to select from a broad product line. Information about the product. Freedom from risk. Installation help. Applications engineering. On-the-job training. Repair service. Image. Status. Prestige. Hope.

WHAT DOES YOUR CUSTOMER WANT?

How can you tell what customers want? Sometimes they will tell you. If they don't, ask them. Sometimes you can't ask prospective customers what they want. Or they can't explain what they are looking for. Or what they say they want doesn't make sense. To answer the question yourself, what will you need? A little research, a little thought—and a lot of listening.

Let's start with the research. Put yourself in your customer's shoes for a few minutes. Suppose that you know a group of young consultants who want an old storefront remodeled into an attractive office. You know that they are on a tight budget and schedule. Where do you start? With a visit to your accountant, your attorney, and your architect friend. Look at their offices and ask them what they like and what they would like to change. Tour your prospective clients' space; take some measurements and make some mental notes. Maybe you're test marketing blackberry chutney and cranberry catsup made from an old family recipe; before you try to sell your preserves to the managers of gift stores and gourmet groceries, walk through their shops. Look at what they carry, how it's packaged, and how it's priced. Watch the people at the cashier; check what products they're buying and how much they seem to be spending.

After you've done the legwork, try the library. The business section can provide information on your customer, the company that he represents, and his industry. For annual sales figures, product names, the names of officers, and the number of employees, check *Standard & Poor's Register*, the *Dun & Bradstreet, Inc. Million Dollar Directory*, and manufacturers' directories. Read the analysts' reports in the *Value Line Investment Survey, The Outlook* from Standard & Poor's Corporation, *Moody's Investors' Service*, and *Standard & Poor's Industry Surveys*. And skim the recent stories in newspapers, trade journals, and news and business magazines. Don't forget annual reports. For information about individuals, ask the librarian for directories like *Who's Who in* the West, *American Architects Directory, Leaders in Educa-tion, Directory of Library Consultants,* and the *New York Times Biographical Service.* Page through unabridged dictio-naries, encyclopedias, and local histories. To learn about the specific problems your client may have, flip back to the news story on her most recent promotion; it may mention why she was appointed. Other sources of information: the librarians at local newspapers, the trade associations to which your client belongs, state reports on planning and economic develop-ment, and instructors at nearby colleges who study certain companies and industries.

Now listen to your customer. Listen to the words he uses and the examples he cites. What does he emphasize? When does he smile? What words does he repeat? Listen for prefer-ences and prejudices. Watch for slumps and shrugs. Most of all, listen to the thoughts and the emotions behind the words and movements. Maybe he's tired; maybe he's depressed. Maybe he had a fight with his boss. Maybe he's afraid—that you're not good enough or that your firm isn't big enough, that he won't like working with you, that you're tempera-mental, that you won't respect his ideas. Maybe he's afraid that you won't deliver on time or on budget. Maybe he's afraid of losing his job. Some customers want more than they say; they want support for proposals they've already made or recommendations that'll unobtrusively move them higher in the office hierarchy. Sometimes they want scapegoats. Some-times they just want people to talk to.

REASSURE YOUR CUSTOMER

From the first telephone call to the final follow-up interview, reassure your customers that you were a wise choice. If they're afraid they won't like working with you, reassure them with charm: make them feel that they are people you want to work with and that you're excited by the opportunity that they are giving you. Be sincere—and be cheerful. If they're concerned that your firm isn't good enough, walk them past your awards certificates and let them page through some of the magazines that have featured your work. If they're worried about how small you are, introduce them to the consultants who are ready to work with you; explain how you tackle rush jobs and unexpected problems. Describe some of the projects that you've handled for firms like theirs. If they're concerned about how much you'll charge, make your presentation complete and accurate but skip expensive-looking paper and embossed printing. Whether you're selling an expensive product or an intangible like a service, quote the research and development costs or the overhead that increases the price; figure out how much this one expensive purchase can save your customers. If they seem afraid that you're not "professional," make sure you act very professional. Bill them accurately and on time. Notify them of any delays with their project and tell them how you're handling the problem. Remember that your customers are human; they respond to image, to ambiance. They favor the people who show them respect and consideration, who understand their problems and their accomplishments. They react to slights and threats.

NEVER STOP SELLING YOURSELF

Never stop selling yourself to your clients. Even after a project's finished and the bills are paid, court clients as you did when you were trying to get their work. Remind them of your skill, your integrity, and your concern for their business. And make your clients feel important, as if they're trusted colleagues you're glad to see again. Greet them with a cheerful "hello" and return their calls promptly; listen to their complaints and answer their questions—or refer them to people who can.

As you read newspapers and magazines, watch for articles that your clients will like. They'll be interested in features on you and your projects, especially when the projects described in the articles are like their own. Don't overlook articles on other topics; if a New York City client asks about your home in the Pacific Northwest, send him or her a copy of an inflight magazine's feature on Seattle. Send an issue of your alumni magazine to the customer whose teenager is applying to college; clip a story on state fairs and festivals for someone new to your area.

When you mail a clipping or a reprint, always add a personal note. Whether you type it on your office stationery or handwrite it on a transmittal form, make the note casual and friendly.

Dear Mr. Brown:

I thought you'd like to see this article on my Bancroft Manor apartment project. As the editor points out, this project was built on a tough site—one with many of the same problems as the lot where you want to build Pine Meadows.

When you write press releases and fact sheets about a project, mention your client unless he or she prefers anonymity. Point out how the client has helped you with the job. When an editor expresses interest in the project, tell your client. When a story about the project is published, call your client with the news. If your project is featured in a magazine, ask the editor to mail an advance copy of the issue to your client with a letter. If the story has appeared in a newspaper, send a clipping to your client with an enthusiastic note. Emphasize how satisfied you are to have the project publicized, even if you're not especially pleased with the details of the story. For example:

Dear Mr. Brown:

Pine Meadows made the papers again! Did you see the story in the Sunday *Gazette*'s real estate page? I'm enclosing a copy of it and of another article that appeared in yesterday's *Courier*. Both stories did a good job of describing the project, although the *Courier* can't seem to spell either one of our names correctly.

Before you order reprints of a magazine feature on your project, ask your client how many copies he or she would like. If the client has never purchased reprints before, suggest two or three ways he or she might use them in business. Remind him or her that you'll both save money if you order the reprints together. If your project is featured in a magazine that conducts readership surveys, ask the magazine editor how well the story on your project was read. If readership was high, either ask the editor to report the survey results in a letter that you can show your client or call your client to describe the high readership.

REPEAT COMPLIMENTS, TOO

Send your clients copies of letters with favorable comments about the projects and repeat any compliments to them.

Dear Mr. Brown:

All sorts of compliments for Pine Meadows! As you can see by the enclosed copy of a letter, the Red Cedar Shingle & Handsplit Shake Bureau is interested in featuring the condominiums in its new product brochure. I'll let you know what the bureau advertising manager thinks of the project after he has had time to study the material I sent him yesterday. By the way, two women stopped in the office yesterday to ask when the units would be going on sale. I gave them your name and number and suggested they call you.

Save the complimentary letters and your early work on a project—the first sketches of a building, the thumbnails for a logo, the Polaroids from a photography job. When the project's completed, compile these in a binder or scrapbook for your client with copies of the press releases, clippings, reprints, duplicates of awards certificates, pictures of the project, and candid photographs of you and your client at the ground breaking, on the shoot, or at the awards presentation.

AWARDS PROGRAMS

Awards programs, which were discussed in more detail in Chapter 9, are excellent marketing tools. With your client's permission, enter awards programs that offer both of you valuable recognition. Tell your client about the programs that you want to enter and ask him or her to suggest others. When you receive an award, send your client a copy of the jury comments on the project. Ask the client for the names of the publications to which he or she would like press releases on the awards sent. If the awards program sponsors don't send press releases to all of these newspapers and magazines, issue the releases yourself.

Ask the awards program sponsors for a duplicate award certificate or plaque for your client; make sure that your client is invited to the awards presentation. Or arrange a special awards presentation in your office (or your client's) with a representative of the awards program. Follow the awards presentation with a reception celebrating the award. This can be a casual Friday afternoon wine tasting, a luncheon, a buffet supper, or an elaborate cocktail party complete with ice sculptures and caviar. Invite your client to bring friends and his or her most important customers and suppliers; the client will be impressed at your courtesy and you'll meet prospective customers in a very flattering setting.

When you enter awards programs and do not win, be gracious. When you report the fact to your client, don't blame anyone and don't accuse the program sponsors or jurors of treating you unfairly. Tell your client how many other projects were entered and mention that every jury makes different choices. If the project can be re-entered in the next year's program, tell your client how you plan to improve your submission. If you need better photography or a more detailed statement from the client, ask for help.

FOLLOW UP!

Make your clients feel that you care about the work you've done for them months and years after the work is done. Call them occasionally to check on their projects. If you design an office building, call your client three or four months after he or she has moved in; ask if the subcontractors finished the final details and if the furniture that you specified is satisfactory. If you planned a direct mail campaign for a firm, ask the marketing manager what kind of response he or she had and what changes he or she would like to make in the next program. Follow up on your customers' complaints, even if the problems aren't your fault. Keep your clients aware of these follow-up efforts, too; send them copies of the letters that you write and memos on the phone conversations.

ENTERTAINING AND GIFTS

Entertaining and gifts are other ways of thanking your customers for their business. However, some companies do not permit purchasing agents and managers to accept anything, even lunches, from suppliers. Other firms require their employees to report anything more than a business lunch. To prevent unflattering comments about you and to limit your expenses, keep your gifts and entertainment tasteful and in proportion to the value of the work that you've received. Plants, cut flowers, and dried flower arrangements are always appropriate thank you, grand opening, anniversary, housewarming, and holiday gifts. You also can send candy, nuts, or a specially decorated cake.

There are many other gifts that your clients will appreciate. If you've designed new stationery for a firm, send the president a pen and pencil set. If you've built a new school, present the principal with a flag for the front lawn or a trophy case for the gymnasium. If you've developed a subdivision, send each new homeowner a subscription to the regional magazine or a festively wrapped armload of fireplace wood. Or print up your own detailed map of the neighborhood, showing shops, schools, churches, and recreational facilities.

When you have a customer with a sense of humor, check into the unusual delivery services available in many larger cities. Send your clients singing telegrams, bouquets of giant balloons, or trios of belly dancers. Remember the unusual when you take customers out to lunch, too. Some clients will be more comfortable in an expensive restaurant or the downtown business club; others may prefer the novelty of a picnic (packed by you or by the corner delicatessen), a stand-up lunch at the local farmers' market, or French onion soup at the gourmet cooking school.

A FINAL WORD . . .

Research, presentations, entertaining, and copies of flattering letters are important tools in developing good client relationships, but none of them are as important as your attitude. If you approach every job as an opportunity, not as an obligation, you'll learn something new and you'll practice your skills. If you treat your customers as the partners they are, if you listen to their suggestions and their questions, you'll discover some very interesting people. Your customers will suggest other jobs for you and other products and services that you should be offering. You'll also learn a lot about yourself and your firm: how you can improve your products and services, how you can increase your sales, and how you can change your selling methods.

APPENDIX A

DIRECTORIES OF PUBLICATIONS

Ayer Directory of Publications, available at many libraries, has more than 100 maps detailed to show the location of every publication listed. Especially helpful when you mail releases to distant communities. Newspapers and magazines are listed by city and state of publication; several indexes cross reference publications by interest and title. Includes college and alumni papers. Order from Ayer Press, 210 W. Washington Square, Philadelphia, PA 19106.

Bacon's Publicity Checker, a two-volume directory with information on both magazines and newspapers, is published annually and is revised three times a year. It includes editors' names and the type of publicity releases used by each publication. Order from Bacon's Publishing Company, 14 E. Jackson Boulevard, Chicago, IL 60604 or call (toll free) (800) 621-0561.

The Design and Building Industry's Publicity Directory, first published in 1980, lists consumer magazines and trade journals that use news and feature stories about development, planning, design, and construction firms. Lists editors' names and indicates how material should be submitted. Sold by The Coxe Letter, c/o MRH Associates, Box 11316, Newington, CT 06111.

Editor & Publisher International Year Book, which is available in libraries or can be ordered each year, lists editorial and advertising information for thousands of daily, weekly, college, and foreign language newspapers. For daily newspapers, the *Year Book* lists editors' names and special editions like the home improvements, parade of homes, and boat show issues. Includes a list of major clipping bureaus. Order from Editor & Publisher, 850 Third Avenue, New York, NY 10022.

Gebbie Press All-in-One Directory lists trade journals, consumer magazines, newspapers, and radio and television stations. It is less detailed than *Bacon's*. To order, write the Gebbie Press, Box 1000, New Palz, NY 12561.

National Newspaper Association, 1627 K Street, Northeast, Washington, DC, sells a list of the state and regional newspaper associations. For the current price, call (202) 466-7200. You can write the associations listed for their membership rosters. Sometimes free, these rosters are valuable sources of information about the small town papers that may not be listed in the national directories.

SRDS Business Publication Rates and Data, published by Standard Rate and Data Service, Inc., is one of several volumes of a monthly directory. Every business journal that subscribes to the service is listed here by title and subject matter; each entry includes a comment on the publication's focus, its advertising rates, and a list of its special editions and advertising deadlines. The book includes the names of firms that accept ads for publishers and publications' geographical and demographic editions. Intended for advertisers, this directory is available at libraries and advertising agencies.

Ulrich's International Periodicals Directory provides information on magazines, especially foreign publications. This information includes the language of publication, publishers' and editors' names, the frequency of publication, and circulation. The addresses given for some of the publications are those of the parent companies, not the editorial offices. Check *Ulrich's* at your library or order a copy from R. R. Bowker Company, 1180 Avenue of the Americas, New York, NY 10036.

APPENDIX B

MORE SOURCES OF INFORMATION

About Writing

The Associated Press Stylebook, The Associated Press, 1977. An alphabetical list of words and expressions with their correct spellings and definitions. Invaluable reference book for anyone. Explains religious beliefs, bond ratings, trade names, titles, and many other terms. Includes Associated Press punctuation rules.

A Manual of Style, The University of Chicago Press, revised twelfth edition, 1969. Written for writers, editors, advertisers, typographers, printers, and proofreaders, this book discusses manuscript preparation, style, and book production. The chapters on style and the detailed glossary of printing and publishing terms are the most valuable for general business use.

Roget's International Thesaurus, by Peter M. Roget, Thomas Y. Crowell Company, fourth edition, 1977. A source of synonyms, antonyms, and related words. It identifies slang and colloquialisms.

The Elements of Style, by William Strunk, Jr. and E. B. White, Macmillan, third edition, 1978. A classic guide to better speech and writing.

Word Watcher's Handbook: A Deletionary of the Most Abused and Misused Words, by Phyllis Martin, David McKay Company, 1976. This book opens with a brief comment on "positive" listening, includes "deletionaries" of trite and overused expressions, and has a chapter on pronounciation "pitfalls." It is witty and easy to read.

The Technique of Clear Writing, by Robert Gunning, McGraw-Hill, revised edition, 1968. First published in 1952, it introduced the Fog Index, a guide to readability.

Gunning's later books include *How to Take the Fog out of Writing* and *New Guide to More Effective Writing in Business and Industry.* Check your library or a bookstore.

The Art of Readable Writing, by Rudolf Flesch, Harper & Row, revised edition, 1974. A guide to making your writing more readable and more interesting. Flesch, who advises you to "keep a running conversation with your reader . . . translate everything into *you* language," also has written several other books. See *How to Be Brief,* published by Harper & Row in 1962, for an alphabetical list of words that can be eliminated from your vocabulary. Also: *The Art of Clear Thinking, The Art of Plain Talk, How to Make Sense, How to Test Readability,* and *How to Write, Speak and Think More Effectively.* Most of these books are short and, because Flesch follows his own advice, interesting.

About Public Relations

"How to Meet the Press," by Chester Burger, *Harvard Business Review,* July-August 1975, pp. 62–70. Guidelines for effective communications with the press. Down-to-earth advice and lots of examples of people who have lost—and won—in confrontations with reporters. If your library doesn't have the *Harvard Business Review* on file, write the Reprint Service, *Harvard Business Review,* Soldiers Field, Boston, MA 02163 or call (617) 495-6192. The minimum order (one to five copies of the same reprint) is $3 for up to five copies.

"What's a PR Director For, Anyway?" by Robert S. Mason, *Harvard Business Review,* September-October 1974, pp. 120–126. Discusses the responsibilities a public relations director should have, what he or she should accomplish, how he or she should be integrated into an existing organization, and how he or she should be evaluated. Mason emphasizes that it's difficult to separate public relations policy from the overall corporate strategy because every major decision has PR implications. The article lists problems some firms have had with PR and the solutions they've found.

"Why New Product Releases Don't Get Published," *Public Relations Journal*, January 1980. This report of a survey of trade publication editors points out that many releases are poorly written or distributed to the wrong magazines. Another major problem: puff.

How to Handle Your Own Public Relations, by H. Gordon Lewis, published by Nelson Hall, 1976. This book covers internal public relations, including telephone manners. There are ideas for many different businesses, from apartment houses and art galleries to beauty salons, burglar alarm sales firms, car dealerships, and camps. It also covers public relations for nonprofit organizations. There are suggestions for publicizing your business in local festivals and with stunts and excellent appendixes with sample press releases.

· *Public Relations for the Design Professional*, by Gerre Jones, McGraw-Hill, 1980. A valuable reference for architects.

About Advertising, Printing, Brochures, and Catalogs

Advertising Copywriting, by Philip Burton, Prentice-Hall, revised edition, 1962. General advice for the copywriter. Sections on specific kinds of writing like retail copywriting.

Advertising Planning & Techniques, by Harland E. Samson, South-Western Publishing Company, 1979. Written as a distributive education workbook, this has step-by-step exercises on advertising programs. Good introduction to radio and television advertising. Budget guidelines are based only on historical industry advertising/sales ratios.

How to Maximize Your Advertising Investment, by Philip M. Johnson, CBI Publishing Company, 1980. Explains advantages and disadvantages of different kinds of advertising; discusses testing, production, and measurement.

The Businessman's Guide to Advertising and Sales Promotion, McGraw-Hill, 1974. Includes brief instructions for producing your own television commercials and designing your own print ads.

Broadcast Advertising: A Comprehensive Working Textbook, by Sherilyn K. Ziegler and Herbert H. Howard, Grid,

Inc., 1978. The section on writing radio commercials includes valuable reminders on the sound of words. It also explains television commercial production and costs and the fee and commission basis for paying advertising agencies.

Television Production Handbook, by Herbert Zettl, Wadsworth Publishing Company, third edition, 1976. Pages of illustrations and examples.

Artists' and Illustrators' Encyclopedia, by John Quick, McGraw-Hill, second edition, 1977. An alphabetical list of technical terms and definitions.

How to Prepare Professional Design Brochures, by Gerre Jones, McGraw-Hill.

Preparing Design Office Brochures: A Handbook, by David Travers, Management Books, 1978.

About Photography

Photography and the Law, by George Chernoff and Hershel Sarbin, Amphoto, fifth edition, 1977. The chapters on ownership of photographs and model releases are especially worthwhile.

The Photojournalist's Guide: Keep the Sun at Your Back, by Arthur H. Bleich and Jerry McCullough, Tech-Data Publications. Good section on "blending," working with your subjects for the best picture. Many examples.

You and Your Prints, by William Hawken, Amphoto, 1978. Very basic guide to photographic prints. Examples illustrate results of using old developer and other errors.

The Step-by-Step Guide to Photography, by Michael Langford, Alfred A. Knopf, 1978. Walks you through every step of photography, from loading the camera and spooling film onto a developing reel to color processing.

About Speaking

An Overview of Speech Preparation, by John Angus Campbell, Modules in Speech Communication Series, Science Research Associates, 1976. Includes a guide to developing topics and organizing speeches. A section on delivery offers suggestions for handling hostile audiences.

About Marketing

"Six Steps to Selling Your Firm's Story," by Joseph A. MacDonald, *SMPS News*, June 1980.

"The Marketing Coordinator," by Janet Goodman, *Interior Design*, May 1980, pp. 94–100. Reprinted in several publications, this article is a valuable description of what a design firm should look for in a marketing coordinator and what responsibilities the coordinator should assume.

"How to Buy and Sell Professional Services," by Warren J. Wittreich, *Harvard Business Review*, March-April 1966, pp. 127–136. Emphasizes three tasks for buyer and seller alike: to identify and minimize uncertainty, recognize and accept the real problem, and deal with each other as professionals.

"Industrial Pricing to Meet Customer Needs," by Benson P. Shapiro and Barbara B. Jackson, *Harvard Business Review*, November-December 1978, pp. 119–127. How to set your price after you understand how much your customer values what he or she is buying. Applicable to services and consumer products as well as to industrial marketing.

"Making the Major Sale," by Benson P. Shapiro and Ronald S. Posner, *Harvard Business Review*, March-April 1976, pp. 68–78. Describes a systematic approach to making complex sales and developing long-term account relationships. For example, the authors tell how to open the selling process and qualify the prospect (how to determine if the prospect really has the interest and ability to buy).

Marketing Architectural and Engineering Services, by Weld Coxe, Van Nostrand Reinhold, 1971. Excellent examples of cold calls and cover letters to prospects. General information on publicity, presentations, direct mail, and brochures.

How to Market Professional Design Services, by Gerre Jones, McGraw-Hill, 1973.

Creative Communications for a Successful Design Practice, by Stephen Kliment, Watson-Guptill, 1977. Not a book on marketing, but a valuable reference for any marketing department. Examples of memos, letters, brochures, press releases, and other written communications. Worth every penny of its price, despite the poor proofreading.

About Your Clients

The Value Line Investment Survey
Standard & Poor's Industry Surveys
Standard & Poor's The Outlook
Moody's Investors Service
Standard & Poor's Register
Dun & Bradstreet, Inc. Million Dollar Directory
The Biographical Dictionaries Master Index
The New York Times Biographical Service
Who's Who
City and manufacturer directories

About Awards Programs

The Design and Building Industry's Awards Directory, The Coxe Letter, c/o MRH Associates, Box 11316, Newington, CT 06111. Lists awards programs for development, planning, and design and construction firms on everything from acoustics and adaptive reuse to water pollution control and windows. It includes a submission checklist.

About Business in General

"Rate Yourself as a Client," by Anthony Jay, *Harvard Business Review*, July-August 1977, pp. 84–92. How to use advisers and consultants. Lists twenty-five principles and pitfalls, including comments on finding and working with consultants and Jay's seven "deadly" sins of advisers and clients. Excellent reminders both for those who consult and for those who hire consultants.

Making It Legal: A Law Primer for the Craftsmaker, Visual Artist and Writer, by Marion Davidson and Martha Blue, McGraw-Hill, 1979. Walks you through the legal problems of starting and operating a business. Covers estimated income taxes, label design, photo releases and rights, copyright, and many other topics. Written with a light touch and lots of examples. If you're going into business, buy it.

APPENDIX C

BASIC SUPPLIES AND EQUIPMENT FOR YOUR PUBLIC RELATIONS ACTIVITIES

General Office

Dictionary: buy a hardbound dictionary that has been revised within the last year or two. Look for one that distinguishes among colloquialisms, slang, and the proper usage of words. Some suggestions: *The American Heritage Dictionary of the English Language, New College Edition; Webster's New World Dictionary, Second College Edition*; and the *Random House College Dictionary.*

Thesaurus: look at the *Roget's* listed in Appendix B.

Style book: *The Associated Press Stylebook* (see Appendix B).

Directory of publications: check the books listed in Appendix A. Buy one directory, take notes from the others in your library, and obtain a list of the weekly and daily newspapers in the states where you do business; from these sources, compile your own mailing list for press releases and feature stories.

Cookbook: *Joy of Cooking*, Irma S. Rombauer and Marion Rombauer Becker, Bobbs-Merrill, 1975. Use the sections titled "Entertaining," "Drinks,"

"Canapes and Tea Sandwiches" and "Hors d'Oeuvres"
to determine how many bottles of wine or liquor to
order for receptions and how many canapes to provide
for each guest. This book illustrates buffet and tea services and tells you how to do everything from curling
butter and garnishing drinks to plugging watermelons
and planning dinners.

Photography

Camera
Tripod
Black-and-white print film and color slide film
Photo pages
File jackets
4 × 5-inch negative preserver manila envelopes
Sleeves for 35mm and $2\frac{1}{4}$-inch negatives and unmounted
    transparencies
Rubber stamps and pad
Adhesive labels in several sizes
Props (see Figure 7-2) and supplies for location shooting
    (see Figure 7-9)

Print Presentations

Dry transfer letters and symbols
Pocket portfolios or presentation folders
Display books

Parties

Invitations
Wine
Hors d'oeuvres
Liquor and ice
Glasses, napkins, and plates
Large wastebasket and garbage bags
Water and mixers

Nonalcoholic beverages
Lemon, lime, and maraschino cherries
Corkscrew and sharp knife
Ashtrays

GLOSSARY

agate type: Small type. Fourteen lines equals one column inch.

aperture: The camera opening that limits how much light reaches the film. Its size is measured in f-stops. The higher the f-stop, the smaller the opening.

bleed: A print that runs to the edge of the page.

booklet: Folded printed material with fewer than forty-eight pages.

Bristol board: Posterboard for general artwork.

brochure: In general, a folder of high quality. Designers call the printed presentations of their work brochures.

broken type: A printed letter that is broken or bent so that white space appears in the middle of the line. Ask your printer to reset lines with broken type.

burnish: To press down on dry transfer letters or cemented artwork to make them adhere to a mechanical.

burnisher: Smooth tool used to press down paste-up material or letters.

C print: Print made from a transparency after an inter-negative has been made.

camera ready copy: Artwork and type that are ready to be photographed for reproduction.

cast-coated paper: Paper with a high gloss coating.

Cheshire label: A kind of mailing label that can be machine applied.

China marker: A pencil with a colored wax center that is used to mark shiny surfaces like photographic paper.

circulation, controlled: The distribution of publications free to qualified professionals and advertisers.

circulation, paid: Distribution of publications by subscription and on newsstands.

clipping bureau: A firm that collects stories on particular topics from hundreds of publications.

coated paper: Paper with a smooth, shiny surface for fine, detailed, and blur-free reproduction.

color separations: *See* separations.

comprehensive: A piece of art that is almost ready for reproduction.

contact sheet: *See* proof sheet.

die cuts: Special shapes (like windows) cut in printed material to create designs or hold business cards.

drilling: Punching holes. It is done in the office with a three-hole punch, at a print ship, and at some quick copy shops.

dry transfer letters: Letters that can be rubbed onto paper or acetate film.

dummy: Page-by-page layout of a book or folder.

editorial calendar: A publication's plan for each issue of the next year or eighteen months.

emboss: To produce raised letters or designs on printed material.

envelope stuffer: Promotional literature mailed with bills. Also called invoice stuffer.

f-stop: A number that measures the size of the aperture, or lens opening, in a camera. Higher f-stops indicate smaller openings and greater depth of field.

flush: Even with. Flush right means even with the right margin or right side of the paper.

foam core: Styrofoam faced with Bristol board. Drawings and photographs can be mounted on foam core.

four-color: *See* one-color.

galley: The long, narrow tray in which metal type stands after being set. Galley proofs are long sheets of paper with the impressions that are taken from the type in the trays.

gatefold: A page that folds out.

glossy finish: A shiny finish on a page or a photo. The opposite of matte.

grain: The distribution of silver particles in the emulsion of films and their images. Small particles create a fine grain and a sharp image.

gutter: The two inner margins of facing pages.

halftones: Gray-toned images in art. The opposite of line cuts.

headline: Large type that "heads" newspaper stories and advertisements.

inverted pyramid: A style of writing in which the most important information comes first.

jargon: Technical language.

justification: Typesetting process in which lines of type are spaced out to a specific measure to produce even margins.

laid paper: Paper with fine parallel and cross lines.

lead: (pronounced leed) The first paragraph or two of a news story. (pronounced led) To insert thin strips of metal, also called leads (pronounced leds), between lines of type to increase the space between them, when using hot type. With the cold type common today, a typesetter leads by allowing space on the camera ready copy.

light box: A small enclosure with a light under a face of glass or plastic. Used for viewing transparencies and in graphic design and printing. Useful for assembling slide presentations.

line cut: A black-and-white drawing. The opposite of halftone.

matte: A dull finish on a page or a photograph.

mechanical: Camera ready art and type; also called a paste-up because all the type and art are pasted into place.

Mylar: A shiny acetate material available in sheets or rolls. Product of E. I. du Pont de Nemours.

news release: *See* press release.

one-color: Printed with one color of ink. The term means that the page goes through the press once. Two-color means two colors of ink and thus two trips through the press. Four- or full-color means four trips through the press and the possibility of a full color spectrum. *See* separations.

padding: Gumming sheets together on one end to make pads. It can be done by a print shop and some quick copy shops.

parallax: The difference in viewing fields of the two lenses of cameras. The view from the viewfinder may be slightly higher than the view from the shooting lens.

paste-up: Camera ready art and type. Also called a mechanical and camera ready copy.

paste-up forms: Bristol board printed with a blue grid. Used for pasting up mechanicals because the blue grid does not appear when the paste-up is photographed.

photostat: High-contrast copy made on a Photostat camera. With a stat you can enlarge or reduce an image.

pica: A standard printing measure indicating one-sixth of an inch or twelve points.

point: A standard printing measure indicating one-twelfth of a pica. Seventy-two points equals one inch.

press release: A short statement distributed to the press by a company or its public relations agency. Also called a news release.

print: (verb) To produce an image on paper or other materials using a press. To make photographic prints. (noun) Photograph.

proof: An inked impression of composed type or of a printing plate.

proof sheet: A sheet of small photographic prints, the same size as the negatives, showing all of the exposures made on a roll of film. Also called a contact sheet.

puff: Flattering, self-serving comments.

R print: A photographic print made directly from a transparency.

ragged left type: Type that is not justified on the left.

ragged right type: Type that is not justified on the right.

ream: A quantity of paper, usually 500 sheets.

register: The correct alignment of color separations. When color separations are out of register, one color is not perfectly aligned with the others and they may overlap. Sunday comic pages are often out of register.

rendering: A perspective drawing of a building or project.

reprints: Copies of already published material. You can buy reprints of editorial features and advertisements from many magazines. Some will lend you their film or plates so that you can have your own reprints made.

reverse: When an image is reversed, it becomes white and the white area around it becomes black or colored.

sans serif type: Type without serifs. Optima is an example.

scout: Someone who sends editors story ideas.

screen print: The reproduction of a photograph or halftone artwork in which the material is broken into a dot pattern.

self-mailer: Direct mail piece that is designed to be mailed without an envelope.

separations, color: The production of plates for process color printing. For full color printing, there are four separations; one plate prints cyan (blue), one magenta (red), one yellow, and one black.

serif: The short, light lines projecting from the top or bottom of letters in type styles like Old English and Bodoni.

shelter magazine: A consumer publication that features the home. *Better Homes and Gardens* is an example.

signature: A group of pages printed on one sheet in such a way that they all fold into the proper sequence, and then are trimmed to form the pages. A signature always has an even number of pages.

sleeves: Protective covers for negatives and transparencies.

subhead: The second headline of a newspaper story or advertisement. It is set in smaller type than the headline.

tear sheet: A page removed from (or never bound into) a book or magazine. Advertisers use tear sheets to check their ads for accuracy and neatness.

trade association: A group, often nonprofit, that represents manufacturers, retailers, or professionals. Its functions may include lobbying, technical service, and promotion. The California Redwood Association is an example.

trade journals: Magazines published for specific trades, industries, or professions. They are often distributed free.

transparency: Color positive film. A transparency is the film that was exposed in the camera and developed. Slides are mounted transparencies.

two-color: *See* one-color.

two-up: Printing flyers, tickets, announcements, and other materials two (or four or eight or sixteen) at a time and then cutting them apart in the trimming process.

INDEX